Jeff Pelizzaro,

D1627162

THE GOLFER'S GUIDE TO A

BOGEY

PROOF

WORKOUT

7 Essentials of a Great Golf Fitness Program

Cover & Interior Design: Lorie DeWorken, MindtheMargins.com

ISBN: 978-1-5327-0852-7

PRINTED IN THE UNITED STATES OF AMERICA

Table of Contents

PREFACE

This book is a not just a guide to playing better golf or designing better golf workouts. The principles in here will ultimately allow you to live a healthier, stronger, and more functional life. It just so happens that, as a result of that, your golf game will be better than it has ever been.

I stress to you that this is a *guide*, plain and simple. It is not a textbook and was not written with the intent of debating philosophies, physiology, biomechanics, kinesiology, or flux capacitors. Instead, you'll find here a collaboration of my own real-world experiences with clients/patients, conversations with some of the best coaches in the world, my own personal fitness experiences, and the successes my colleagues and I have had using these principles.

If you implement the strategies and foundational ideas in this book, you will be well on your way to the best golf you've ever played and a much healthier lifestyle.

I hope you enjoy it.

Jeff

INTRODUCTION

The fact that you are reading this book tells me a few things about you. The most obvious of the bunch is that you:

A. like to play golf

and

B. you most likely work out.

Brilliant, right? Especially because the words "golf" and "fitness" are both in the title of this book. But, beyond knowing those simple facts about you, I'm going to venture a couple of other assumptions of mine which likely describe you in one way or another.

For instance, I would bet that you aren't just your run-of-the-mill, average golfer who likes to play with his buddies every now and again. I am guessing that you play a couple of times per week (or at least would like to), you play pretty competitively, and you do not take kindly to losing, even if it is just with your friends for a couple of bucks.

I'm also going to make the assumption that you're on some sort of a workout regimen, or, if not, you have been in the past. It may have been as far back as college or when you were involved in a sport at a younger age, but you realize that your performance level was at its highest when you were challenging your body on a fairly high level. You're looking to get that **EDGE** back in your golf game.

If that doesn't quite fit your description, you just might, like many of my clients, have been working for many years, possibly behind a desk or behind the wheel. You likely are now a golf addict, but realize that your body just won't respond the way it used to and the only way to make big improvements in your swing and game is to get your body moving better.

Am I right? Does any of this sound at all like you?

Good. I just want to make sure that I have the right audience for the information that is in this book.

I'd like to introduce myself: I'm Jeff Pelizzaro, physical therapist, golf fitness professional, and co-founder of **18STRONG.com** and the **18STRONG Podcast.**

My mission in creating these platforms (along with this book) is to compile information and content to help golfers like you live a stronger life and play a stronger game. On our website/podcast I am able to bring you not only lessons from my own personal experiences, but also lessons from some of the greatest coaches around the world.

It is my honor to guide you on this tour of some of the most essential things that you should be doing in your fitness program. And possibly more importantly, help you avoid some of those things you may have been told to do, which are likely sabotaging your performance in the gym and on the course.

Over the years, I've had the opportunity to work with hundreds of golfers, as well as interview and connect with some of the greatest coaches in the golf world. Not only has it been incredible to work with so many great people, but, also in that time, I have seen and learned A LOT.

WHAT YOU'RE GOING TO GET

Just as we promise in our content on **18STRONG.com,** I don't want to waste your time with a bunch of useless info and fluff that you don't need or care about in this book. I intend to simply get to the point of each topic, give you some good resources, and provide you with an action plan to get started immediately.

In this next section, I am going to lay out exactly what you can expect from this book. However, for the sake of efficiency, if you would rather get right into the meat of this guide, just skip ahead to the section titled "Learning From the Best" on page 9.

A DETAILED DESCRIPTION

A description of some of the most important elements I see the top coaches and players implementing into their routine

A Solid Plan of Attack

Without a plan, you may as well accept the fact that your gains will be minimal and you'll likely never get stronger, hit a ball farther, or score significantly better. EVER.

A More Balanced Program

Without taking this into consideration, you will likely over-train some muscle groups and under-train others. This recipe for injury can EASILY be corrected.

Excellent Nutritional Strategies

Most people THINK they eat "pretty" well. Most people are **WRONG**. If you are serious about looking better and using nutrition as an advantage for your game, I have some fundamentals that you need to know about. These include:

- everyday eating guidelines
- pre/post-workout nutrition
- supplements that are actually worth your $

Quality of Execution

At **18STRONG.com** we believe that every exercise and every rep count. Thus, it's imperative that you treat each movement with the same respect regarding posture, tempo, and mental focus as you would if you were on the first tee at Augusta.

This also goes for each program and workout you design. You should have a reason as to why you are doing each exercise (or golf drill), not just because you read about it in some magazine.

A Willingness to Challenge Yourself

Without challenging yourself by incorporating bigger, better, and smarter lifts/exercises into your routine, you greatly limit your potential.

Strength x Speed = Power
(Actually, the real definition is Work/Time = Power,
to get technical.)

Without the strength part, you can't generate the almighty POWER that you are ultimately after.

Smarter Cardio

Over the past decade or more, there has been a huge rise in the popularity of using low to moderate intensity cardio exercise as a primary focus for exercise. As a golfer (and, in my opinion, in most situations) this type of cardio is highly inefficient in producing results for fat loss, power development, and overall health benefits. I'll show you several other ways that are way more productive and time friendly.

The Ultimate Game Changer

Are you ready for it? The secret mistake that almost everyone makes? Here it is:

Not Having a GREAT Mentor or Coach!

Are you disappointed? I know I was when I first got this advice. All that hype, and that's it? "C'mon, Jeff, you've gotta have something better than that, right?" WRONG.

Trust me; this IS the most important one.

Read on, and I'll explain why.

A FEW OF OUR BEST RESOURCES

I want to make sure this book doesn't just get read, but becomes one that you USE. In saying that, I feel obligated to give you some tools which will really help you get moving in the right direction. I'll name a few of the resources that you have coming to you just for taking the time to read this:

- Our nutrition guidelines

- A downloadable workout template to use to design your own programs

- A complete four-week strengthening program to get you started and create a solid base for your future performance

- Sprint Training Protocols for golfers to make sure you know how to properly integrate high intensity intervals into your program

- **The 18STRONG Podcast**: I have to mention this one because this provides an endless resource of interviews with THE BEST coaches, trainers, and players in the world. And it only continues to grow.

- **18STRONG.com**: Like the podcast, this resource continues to grow. It is the home base for all of our content, including podcasts, articles, and videos created by me and other well respected authorities in the golf and fitness world.

YOUR ACTION PLAN

Let me be frank. The information in this book isn't worth a damn if you don't take action on it. So I want to make it as easy as possible for you to start getting things done when it comes to your new Golf Fitness Program.

By the end of this course. . .

- You will know exactly how to prevent mistakes from ever creeping back into your program so you can maximize every workout and break through your fitness plateaus.

- You will have a better grasp on the principles of a great training program and will know more than the majority of other golfers (and even trainers).

- You will have access to the tools not only to start the program that I've designed for you, but you also will be able to create your own plans to continually take your game and your body to the next level.

Now, let's get this party started.

LEARNING FROM THE BEST

I've seen a lot of things in the gym over the years, both good and bad. And I'll be the first to admit that I've been the one doing some of the good—and definitely some of the BAD.

That's the way life goes: we do stupid things; we learn that it was a mistake, and, hopefully, we make the changes to do it better next time. I believe that's the way good coaches, players, students, etc., become great.

That is why I am never too quick to ridicule or dismiss someone for doing the wrong thing in the gym or trying something new. That's how we learn our best lessons. This section is a simple reminder that we should always look for ways to get better, even if it means admitting that what we've been doing for years is either wrong, outdated, or simply not the most effective method.

Need an example? One that comes to mind is the fascination with the use of instability devices in training. You may have seen a very famous golfer on the cover of a magazine at one point, standing on an exercise ball, swinging a golf club. While the photo intrigues and documents a pretty fascinating accomplishment, it constitutes, in my personal opinion, a non-effective and, very risky exercise.

(I would've put a copy of that photo here, but I'm pretty sure I would be breaking some sort of copyright law, so just search for "golf swing on exercise ball," and I'm sure you'll find it.)

As I mentioned, we are all guilty of doing or trying something like this, so there is nothing of which to be ashamed. The important thing here is that we can learn better, safer, and less risky ways to improve our performance.

When I switched over from practicing as a clinical physical therapist to working strictly in the strength and conditioning/golf fitness world, I assumed that, based on my background and schooling, I knew more than most of the trainers around whom I was working.

When I saw some of the exercises that some of the strength coaches were using and how they trained their clients, I thought they were crazy. Some of the thoughts that crossed my mind included:

- Why are they using so much weight?

- Why are they letting their knees go in front of their toes?

- Why is he squatting so low?

- Isn't that bad for their backs?

- Why would a golfer need to do that exercise—it doesn't look like a golf swing?

- They should be doing more balance and unstable surface training.

- Can't they get just as much benefit with body-weight exercises?

- And many more. . .

But what I've come to realize in the last 5+ years of working with and learning from some of the best strength coaches around is that I honestly knew very little about true strength training and performance enhancement.

I knew what a good physical therapist knows and did a very good job in the rehab world, working with injured clients and getting athletes back on their feet, and competing in their sport. But when it came to real development of strength, power, and sport-specific training, I was in a whole new world.

Once I realized that, I put my ego aside and decided to start soaking up as much knowledge as I could. I started to get myself around the best of the best. I partnered up and began a sports performance company with one of the most experienced strength coaches in hockey, and I started going to seminars, reading books, and simply learning as much as I could since I took the first step on this journey.

I have since learned that if you simply watch what the **smart, successful** people do and follow their lead, guess what: you've stepped onto the path to becoming smart and successful yourself. The same philosophy definitely applies to YOUR golf game.

And that is where *The Golfer's Guide to a Bogey Proof Workout* comes into play. All of those mistakes that I've made and the lessons I've learned (and continue to learn), have now become a resource for you and thousands of other golfers. (And the lessons continue to increase with all of the new interviews, videos and articles that we release on our site at **18STRONG.com** on a weekly basis.)

There's no sense in your making the same mistakes I have. Why waste your time going through it all, when you can learn from what I've been through? Think of this as your golfers' "CLIFF NOTES." I've sifted through the BS for you, giving you a head start on your journey.

Now let's get into the meat of what you came for which is:

The 7 Essentials of a Great Golf Fitness Program

#1
A SOLID PLAN OF ATTACK

I f you don't have a plan, you're in trouble.
Plain and simple.

I had a client a couple of years ago, a younger guy with a full-time job and four kids. Needless to say, he was a busy man, but he loved golf and wanted to start competing at a higher level. He knew his fitness and mobility level needed some help so he contacted me.

After evaluating him and figuring out what he needed, we put together a training program for him to do on his own that addressed some of the most important things he needed. The **PLAN** boiled down to some basic strengthening, mobility work, and some weight loss. He had 3 separate workout designed specifically for him to perform each week along with a few stretches/corrective exercises to work on some of his problem areas.

We worked together a couple of times, but he didn't seem able to keep a consistent workout routine and just didn't follow the plan. After our third or fourth meeting, he didn't come back.

Six months to a year later, I heard from him again, and he asked me what I thought about a very popular group-exercise type of workout that he was doing. I warned him that I would not recommend it, based on our previous conversations regarding his golf goals.

Unfortunately, he did not follow my advice. It was more convenient for him to drop into a class here and there when his schedule allowed, and he "felt" like he was getting a great workout.

But something happened. His body started hurting, and his golf game did not get better. He began to realize that the inconsistent workouts and generalized routine he was doing did not provide what **HIS** body needed. He was not getting any closer to his goals. His workout schedule had become very haphazard with no real direction.

When he finally called again, we got to work. We put together another program that he found manageable with his schedule, and he stuck to it. He knew what he was supposed to do, how many times a week, and had some goals in mind.

Within a month he noticed big improvements in how his body felt and how he was hitting the ball. He told me it was the best he had felt in a long time. In fact, his game improved quite a bit, and he competed at a very high level in his next tournament. Unfortunately, he just missed out on qualifying for a national tournament in a sudden-death playoff.

What was the difference?

Well, there were several keys to his success, but they all stem from having a plan of attack. He was more focused and diligent about getting in his workouts. He stuck to a more consistent schedule. And he made the necessary changes to his body that allowed him to play better.

And I would say that every bit of this began with the simple fact that we had a plan for him. He knew his goals, he knew what his workout schedule needed to be and he was more prepared each week to get the work done that needed to get done!

WHAT'S IN A GOOD PLAN?

By "plan" I mean a fairly specific, **written-out** program that you intend to follow. This should also include written goals, even if they are something as general as:

- "driving the ball 10 yards farther"
- "losing 10 lbs."
- "gaining 5 lbs. of lean body mass"
- "working out 4 times per week"

The important thing is that you have something that you work toward.

A good plan is more than just a written out workout program. To really make it solid and effective in getting you closer to your goals, it should have three components to it:

1. Consistency
2. Progress
3. Accountability

Let's look at each in a little more detail.

Consistency

Without consistency, all hope for any program flies out the window. (*NOTE: This is one of those that you might want to write down. In fact, this may be the number one, most important thing you get out of this entire book.*) If you are not consistent in your efforts—be that practicing, eating well, training on a regular basis—then you can't expect to create any significant, long-lasting changes in your fitness level or your game.

You need to create habits and lifestyle changes. Otherwise, yes, you may experience short bursts of success, but the changes will not be permanent.

As mentioned, the best place to start is to follow a written program. This goes for your diet, too, which we'll get into later, but, for now, let's focus on the workout program.

Too often I see golfers wandering around the gym, searching out the next exercise they are going to do, kind of like standing in the kitchen with the refrigerator door open looking for a snack—not exactly a well thought-out workout.

If your workout routine looks like this, you're in trouble.

If no structure or strategic plan of attack exists, a workout like this will fall short. Randomly throwing together a workout every time you go to the gym means you will forget some important components, or you will find yourself in a rut, repeating the same exercises time and again.

In contrast, when you have a written out program, you know exactly when, why, and how much you expect to do on any given day and, thus, will much more likely follow through. If you don't have that kind of a written commitment, some days you'll feel like really getting after it, but other days you'll skip out.

How many times have you had a long day at work, and, when you got to the gym, those weights just looked too heavy so you opted for a light "cardio day," maybe a few stretches, and then you went on your way home to eat dinner and catch up on "Breaking Bad" on Netflix?

When you have a defined program, that doesn't happen. You have an agenda. You know what you need to do each day. Your conscience is too strong. The guilt is too powerful. You know that Monday is leg day, and whether you like it or not, you have to squat a ton of weight, or you won't be able to find peace in order to sleep that night.

You know it's gonna be tough, but you still do it. That's where the magic is.

When you have that kind of structure, you'll find yourself committed to completing each workout. As you start to groove that routine, you'll start to see the changes as the weeks go by. Your strength will improve dramatically; your body will start to change, and you'll get to check those goals off of what previously was more of a "wish list" than a list of real "goals."

Simply by being consistent and having a program to which you are committed, you've entered the road to change and progress.

Progress

Speaking of progress, one simple trick can speed it up.

Have you ever started a workout program or really gotten into a practice routine for your golf game but felt as if progress was not being made? It happens all the time.

In most cases, however, I find that there is a very simple answer to this lack of progress.

Believe it or not, the one thing that will skyrocket your progress in the gym is simply:

Writing Down How Much You Lift.

I know, it may not be the ancient Chinese secret you expected. It seems like common sense, but I'm always surprised at how many people I see in the gym working out without a program and NOT documenting their exercises, weights, and reps from week to week.

I guess I can't fault them, though, because I used to act the same way. But once I started writing every lift and exercise down, always trying to get better on the next set or in the next workout, it made a huge impact on my strength, as well as my mental approach at training.

Why would you not want to know how you did last week and want to improve on it this week?

I'll give you an example of the effects of writing down the weights. I have a client that I've been working with for a while now. He is in his early 50's and when he first came to see me, he had been working out for several years in the gym, but never had a real program and never wrote down any of his weights.

He was a slave to the same routine for years which generally included the elliptical, some dumbbell presses, some curls and a few other random exercises.

In the course of the 5+ years that he did this "program," he never went above 25lbs. on a dumbbell chest press. But since we started working together and we keep track of the weight he lifted last week, he was recently able to perform 8-10 reps of incline dumbbell presses at 50lbs.

I would like to say it's all because of my amazing skill as a coach, but I attribute most of it to the fact that we keep track of his weight lifted and know that we can try to push a little more each day, week, or month.

He simply didn't do this before, so he always defaulted back to the weight he knew he could lift. If he only would've paid attention to this years ago, imagine the gains he could have made.

I figure if you are reading this, there is a 99% chance that you have a very competitive side and this concept of always improving should be right up your alley. Doesn't it bother you if you've been putting in all of this effort and you don't see yourself getting better, stronger, leaner, etc.? It should. But you'll never know if you don't keep track.

You don't have to make massive gains each week. The important thing is that you push yourself each and every time you step foot into that smelly gym. Always strive to add a few pounds, get a few more reps, or simply do an exercise with a little more ease and better form each time you're in there.

Accountability

If you've never had a real workout partner, this section may be a game-changer for you. Accountability can be one of the most powerful driving forces in any fitness program, and I find the best way to hold yourself accountable is simply to make someone else do it!

Seeing that you have read this far tells me that you have the desire to get better and, thus, most likely have a good amount of willpower when it comes to sticking to your workouts.

Either way, even if you do have a pretty good track record of sticking with your workouts (and diet), I have found no stronger motivator than having someone else in the trenches with me.

Ask a buddy, a coach, a girlfriend, whatever, but when you have someone else encouraging you to get to the gym on those days when you don't quite feel up to the task, you'll not just let yourself down, you'll let that other person down, too. In my experience, it's this thought of disappointing your accountability partner that often forces you to suck it up and get the job done.

My personal preference is to find someone who has similar goals to yours so you can work out together, eat similar diets, etc. This way you both know each other's pain and can push each other on when one of you doesn't feel up for the challenge.

It's easy to say, "I'm not quite feeling it today," and put it off till tomorrow when you are in it by yourself. But when you have a partner willing to do the work with you, you'll find it much more difficult to bail on him/her and still feel like a man when your head hits the pillow that night.

Another way I could put it for those of you who love motivational quotes is...

"Accountability: guilt yourself into the best shape of your life!"

The word "**guilt**" typically has a negative connotation, but you can also use it as a very powerful tool and motivator. If you don't do what you say you're going to do and someone calls you out on it, you have two possible reactions.

You either:

1. **Man up and do what you said you would**

   or

2. **Make an excuse not to do it.**

And unless you are some cold, heartless monster, you will most likely feel guilty when you go back on your word.

BOGEY-PROOF ACTION TIPS FOR CREATING A SOLID PLAN

- Write out a training program or have one written out for you. It should break up your week into several workouts so you know what day you do each workout.

- Commit to doing it for 4-6 weeks straight without cheating.

- Write down every weight lifted for each workout and make an effort to improve at least every week (even if only by a couple of pounds).

- Find a partner. If he/she can't work out with you, find a partner who will actually get on your butt when you don't do what you say—not someone who will let you slide. This is IMPERATIVE!!!!!

Find these tips and more at BogeyProofWorkout.com/resources.

A MORE BALANCED PROGRAM #2

Balance is often noted as the most important task of the body on a cellular level. Our bodies always look to find balance chemically, nutritionally, mentally, spiritually, and physically. It's a constant battle that can never be completely achieved. But, when we are way out of balance, bad things happen: we get sick; we fall down; we get stressed; etc.

With such a strong, natural, primitive urge, I find it interesting how lopsided we tend to get in our workout programs and as a result, our bodies.

I guess in some ways it makes sense, given the fact that some of the situations mentioned above lie on more of a subconscious level. But, when it comes to things that we have more conscious control over (i.e., our training programs, diet, etc.), we often lean towards simply doing what we like and what seems convenient, as opposed to what may be more beneficial in the long run.

For instance, how often do you see guys in the gym working on the bench press, arm exercises, and their abs? Quite a bit. Contrast that with how often you see them working on pull-ups, low back exercises, posture, and hamstrings. Not so much.

We tend to do the things we like to do or that we are good at, but what you also need to include are the ones that you are a little afraid of, the hard ones, the ones that make you not want to go to the gym. Those are the exercises that are going to make you better than you are today.

Here's a short list of some of the exercises that tend to get "overlooked":

- pullups
- deadlifts
- squats
- glute ham raises
- back extensions
- rotator cuff exercises
- posture exercises
- non-dominant side exercises
- foam rolling
- flexibility/mobility exercises
- sprints (or high intensity intervals)
- anything mid-, low-, or upper-back related.

Do you see a pattern in these? Often these exercises relate to the back side of the body, otherwise known as the "posterior" or "posterior chain."

Our lives have become so front-side dominant due to our daily activities of sitting at a desk, driving a car, watching TV, and doing everything in a forward pattern such that our bodies naturally start to round forward and tighten in these positions.

Next time you are in a public place with lots of people, look around and make a note of the sitting and standing postures of those in the crowd. Most likely you'll see a lot of slouching, rounded shoulders, forward heads, and people hunched over their mobile phones.

Because of this, YOU MUST make a conscious effort to counteract this, keeping your body strong, flexible, and BALANCED in all directions to optimize your physical and sports-related capabilities.

In the next few sections we'll cover a few simple guidelines that you can implement which will get you on the right track.

I recommend that you start looking at your workouts in a more systematic fashion. Each one should accomplish a goal, and every exercise in that individual workout should have its role and place.

Gone are the days of simply throwing together 5-8 random exercises and doing something different every time you step in the gym. While that can seem entertaining and more creative, when you have no structure or blueprint, you'll get very little results.

By "blueprint" I mean a general design that guides your program. Just like putting together a plan to build a high rise, you have to make sure the foundation gets laid properly and you have all your supplies accounted for. Otherwise, you'll end by picking up the rubble on the street in a few years.

PUSH vs. PULL

As you are just getting into designing your programs, I suggest you start here. Think of your exercises as either a general pushing exercise or a pulling exercise and split them up evenly in your workout.

For example, bench presses and squats are pushing exercises, whereas pull-ups and deadlifts are pulling exercises. The idea is not to overdo one or the other. Balance them out.

Your **quadriceps (quads) and chest** exercises are typically going to be executing more of a pushing movement (pushing weight away from your center), and your **hamstrings/glutes and back** exercises are usually more of a pulling movement (toward the center of your body).

It amazes me to see the discrepancy between the push and pull strength of individuals. I've worked with some who are extremely push-dominant, as well as with others who are definitely more "pullers."

For example, one of my clients could bench press over 300 lbs., but couldn't get a legit pull-up if his life depended on it until we balanced out his workouts and really emphasized the pulling movements.

While your body style may always prefer one direction or the other, the goal is to close the gap. The smaller the gap, the less chance your body will resort to compensations in movement and, thus, the less risk of injury.

Quick Note: While there are definite exceptions to these principles depending on the overall goals of one's program, we are going to keep it simple for now so you can get in the habit of using the basic fundamentals when designing a program. Overtime, you'll be able to play around a little more with these concepts.

See the chart below for a short list of examples of push vs. pull exercises.

PUSH	VS.	PULL
• Squats		• Deadlifts
• Leg Press		• Hamstrings Curls
• Split Squats		• Back Extensions
• Lunges		• Good Mornings
• Step Ups		• Reverse Hyperextensions
• Bench Press		• Glute/Ham Raises
• Push Ups		• Bridges
• Incline Press		• Pulldowns
• Flies		• Pull Ups/Chin Ups
• Shoulder Press		• Reverse Flies
• Dips		• Rows
• Triceps Extensions		• Biceps Curls
• Quads-Dominant Exercises		• Hamstrings/Glutes-Dominant Exercises
• Chest-Dominant Exercises		• Back-Dominant Exercises

For videos on these exercises and more, you can go to:

BogeyProofWorkout.com/resources

to watch and download all of the resources from this book.

BIG vs. SMALL

Some exercises give you more bang for your buck in regards to how much work gets done, how much weight you can lift, and how many body parts you can train in the movement. Some exercises are more isolated and specific for different muscle groups or movements.

All of these exercises have their place and function, but how you do them in your program can greatly affect the quality of each training session and the residual benefits afterwards.

For instance, if you are working your legs, you wouldn't want to do a bunch of calf-raises at the beginning of the workout before you do your squats or deadlifts. Your calves would be exhausted which would severely decrease the quality of the other "bigger" exercises.

To create a little more clarity regarding exercises, I'd like to break down the different exercises in a program into four basic categories:

1. **Primary**: These exercises I would call the "BIG" ones. They include multiple joints, often multiple planes of movement, and larger movement patterns. For these, free weights are used to create the highest stimulation of not just the muscles, but also of the central nervous system (e.g., barbell squats, deadlifts, bench press, pullups).

2. **Secondary**: These are similar to the primary exercises, but do not create quite as much demand on the central nervous system. In general, these exercises do not involve as much weight or may involve a machine such as the leg press (e.g., lunges, glute-ham raises, dumbbell bench presses, lat pulldowns).

3. **Auxiliary/Isolation**: These exercises are geared to target a specific muscle group. This category contains a much larger number of exercises that create a significantly lower demand on the central nervous system. Often referred to as "isolation" exercises, they

require much less weight and usually only involve a small number of joints in the movement. Most weight machines will fall into this category (e.g., hamstring curls, step-ups, flies, biceps curls, triceps extensions).

4. **Corrective**: This category, a little different from the others, is more about changing or correcting movements, restrictions, and strength imbalances which may hinder performance in the other areas. Thus, depending on how you look at it, some argue that this group is the most important component of a program because they prime you to do the "bigger" exercises properly.

This group includes flexibility exercises, rehab, stabilization drills, movement patterns, proper sequencing of movements, and muscle-firing patterns (e.g., stretching, balance exercises, golf positions, swing-sequence drills).

See the chart on the next page for more examples of these types of exercises.[1]

Please note that this is not a comprehensive list, just a list of familiar exercises to give you an idea of where some of these would be classified. Also note that classifications can overlap.

Knowing the difference between the different kinds of exercises will make you much more efficient in designing a program that's right for you. While this may not seem like an earth-shattering lesson, just by placing your exercises in the right order, I guarantee you will see an improvement in your quality of workouts, as well as your strength gains over the course of the program.

---

1. Reference: "How to Design a Damn Good Program—Part 1" by Christian Thibaudeau, www.t-nation.com.

CLASSIFICATION of EXERCISES (examples)

PRIMARY

Lower Body

- Barbell Squats, Front Squats, Barbell Deadlifts, Romanian Deadlifts

Upper Body

- Bench Press, Barbell Shoulder Press, Military Press, Pull-ups, Chin Ups, Bent Over Barbell Rows, Chest-Supported Rows, Barbell Curls, Close-Grip Barbell Press, Dips

SECONDARY

Lower Body

- Lunge, Split Squats, Hack Squats, Dumbbell (DB) Squats, Step Ups, Good Mornings, Glute-ham Raises, Hamstring Curls, Back Extensions

Upper Body

- Incline Bench Press, DB Bench Press, DB Incline Press, One-arm DB Rows, Pull Downs, Seated Cable Rows, DB Curls, Zottman Curls, Incline Close-Grip Press, DB Triceps Extension

AUXILIARY

Lower Body

- Step Ups, Knee Extensions, Hamstrings Curls, Reverse Hyperextensions, Swiss Ball Exercises

Upper Body

- Dumbbell Flies, Cable Flies, Push Ups, Chest Press Machines, Cable Pullovers, Dumbbell Pullovers, Machine Rows, Straight Arm Pulldowns, Cable Curls, Overhead Triceps Extension, Cable Triceps Extensions

CORRECTIVES

- Rolling Patterns, Calf/Ankle Stretches/Mobilization, Foam Rolling, Band-Assisted Exercises, Proprioception Exercises, Hamstring Stretches, Trunk-Rotation Exercises, Trunk/Hip-Rotation Mobility, Sequencing Patterns, Muscle-Activation Techniques, Soft-Tissue Mobilization, ART, DNS, this list is endless . . .

With these categories in mind, you need to utilize the primary and some-times secondary exercises first in your workouts.[2] This ensures that your muscles and nervous system operate at their freshest, ready to respond and to produce the best results.

After that, you will move more into the secondary and auxiliary exercises to target your desired areas a little more specifically. I think of them as "add-ons," or, as one fellow coach describes them, they are like the "icing on the cake."

In general, I like to think of it as moving from **BIG** to **small.**

As for the corrective exercises, this group stands alone by themselves. Depending on how much time you have, you can do these before the workout, after the workout, and even on your off days.

I would suggest that you not do too much before your workout. Again, you want your muscles and joints as fresh as possible going into your first lifts. Therefore, I would only do a couple correctives which will directly help facilitate a better movement or range of motion for the movement patterns that you will work on in that session.

For example, if you tend to have tight hamstrings, you may want to do a light warm-up to get them ready on a day that you plan to do deadlifts. Or, if you have chronically tight calves, you may want to foam roll them out to allow for fuller range in your squats.

But working on your ankle mobility and rolling out your quads before an upper-body-dominant strength session will not do you much good and will just drain some of the energy that you should save for your lifts.

Often, I will give my clients corrective exercises as "homework," for them to work on after their workouts AND at home. Because these

2. *Note: At times programs will vary from this, depending on the intention of the program and the training level of the individual.

are movements and stretches that are meant to break bad habits and improve mobility, they should be done on a much more frequent basis (often daily, or at least multiple times a week).

Delving into the corrective exercises in depth could be an entire book in itself so we will save that for another day.

LEFT VS. RIGHT

Next, in this conversation about "balance" we come to the "dominant versus nondominant side." It's no surprise that most of us are either right-side or left-side dominant. We write, throw, and kick better with one limb compared to the other. Subsequently, we also swing a club better in one direction than another.

We often exhibit a difference in our strength, both in isolated movements and in more compound movements. This can cause problems in sport, especially when starting a new training program.

Think about how many swings you've made with your golf club—all of them in the same direction, mind you. Do you think that hasn't jacked up your body a bit? Do you ever swing the club the other way? If not, you definitely should.

Similarly, we tend to do everything else with our dominant side which results in decreased strength, mobility, stability, and coordination on the opposite side.

Imbalance leads to injury. Our bodies take the path of least resistance which means we will compensate when faced with physical activities that challenge us. If a body part is stiff, another joint will often move excessively to make up for the limitation. If a muscle is not activating properly or isn't strong enough to perform a task, another muscle/tendon/joint will pick up the slack.

While this is good in the sense that the body gets the job done no matter what, it's still bad in the sense that other parts of the body have to sacrifice for the one body part that won't function properly.

When you start to add loads to the body as you do in a training program, you need to gain an awareness of these imbalances and combat them rather than making them worse.

Here are two suggestions on how you can combat this:

1) ALWAYS work your weaker/non-dominant side first in any unilateral exercises.
To be clear, this means, if you are doing an exercise that works primarily one side at a time, such as single arm presses, split squats, single arm rows, etc. you should start with your weaker side on every set.

Again, because you will be coming off of your rest from the last set, this allows your brain and body to function at their sharpest and freshest when working that side of the body as opposed to being tired. This, in turn, allows you to learn the movements faster and recruit the muscles more efficiently than if you felt slightly fatigued.

It may sound silly, and you're probably thinking, "Does it really matter?" Well, the answer is YES. It ABSOLUTELY does. Your brain and body are amazing in their capacity to learn and function. Every advantage we can give counts.

A second way to close the gap between the weak and strong side is to . . .

2) Let the weaker side dictate the weight and number of reps performed.
For instance, if you do a rotator cuff exercise on the left side with a 12-lb. weight and you can only perform nine reps, then you would only do nine reps of the same weight on the right side (even though you may feel as though you could do 15).

This simply prevents the right side from getting too far ahead of the left. In fact, you could even speed the process up a little by ending with an extra set on the weak side. When your exercises are executed properly and you use these techniques, it won't be long before the weak side catches up, and you can proceed without these concerns.

ROTATION EXERCISES

Rotation drills are generally the favorite of the golfer, and in my experience can often be overdone. Yes, golf is a rotational sport, and yes, we need to work on these movements, but in many cases, I see golfers jump into these exercises too quickly.

My buddy Jason Glass has a great quote that I steal all of the time, "you have to earn the right to rotate." This basically means that we need to make sure you can move and stabilize other parts of your body in more simplistic patterns first, then we can venture into the rotation, which is a much more complicated pattern for the body.

With that being said, I understand that the rotation exercises are often more fun than the others. Throwing medicine balls and mimicking the golf swing with weights or cables can give the impression that you are specifically working on your game, even when you're not on the course. But I caution you here; DO NOT go overboard on the rotational exercises. In general, I will put in one or two specific rotational exercises in a given workout, but only if I know that we have covered some of the basics and main objective movements of that particular workout.

In most cases, I would recommend saving most of the abdominal or core-related rotational exercises toward the end of the workout, especially if the rest of the workout included any heavy lifting or neurologically taxing movements.

A program focused too much on the rotation aspect of the game is often lacking some of the more fundamental movements such as the squat, deadlift, lunge, press, and pull. Thus, this is just a word of caution to not get too carried away with this group of exercises, especially because they really do tend to be more fun!

When you do add in a rotational exercise, make sure you perform it on both sides of the body. Believe it or not, there are some golfers that only want to do an exercise if it mimics their golf swing, and thus, if an exercise looks or feels like their backswing, they don't see the benefit of doing that drill, exercise on both sides of the body. This is a HUGE mistake, as you now know based on everything we talked about above.

I hate to be a broken record, but make sure you are treating both sides of the body the same. As you start working your non-dominant side more, I promise you will start to see an improvement in your balance over the ball and throughout out your swings from tee to green.

BOGEY-PROOF ACTION TIPS FOR A MORE BALANCED PROGRAM

- Figure out which exercises you tend to skip and commit to putting them in your next several programs.

- Identify the **PUSHING** and **PULLING** exercises in your program and break them up evenly in the course of your program.

- Start your workouts with one or two **BIG** exercises to which you feel you can give every ounce of intensity you have, and then decide on several **smaller** exercises to support those.

- ALWAYS start your unilateral exercises **on the weaker side** and let that side determine your weight/load and number of reps.

- Start swinging the golf club in the opposite direction to improve flexibility and overall coordination (this will inevitably help your real swing).

- Add in some rotational exercises into your workout, just make sure they do not dominate your program.

Find these tips and more at BogeyProofWorkout.com/resources.

EXCELLENT NUTRITION STRATEGIES #3

G olfers are now starting to see the benefits of getting in the gym and working hard, but I am still often shocked at how many bad decisions are made away from the gym, namely at the dinner table and especially on the 19th Hole (otherwise known as the bar!).

Don't get me wrong; growing up in St. Louis, Missouri, the home of Budweiser beer, toasted Ravioli, and gooey butter cake (doesn't that just sound amazing?), I love a good beer and delicious food as much as the next guy. But you have to realize that, no matter how hard you work in the gym, the old adage is true. . .

"You can't out-train a bad diet."

Therefore, if you really want to make a change, it's going to require a real commitment. I don't know who gets credit for the above quote, but if you've ever tried to lose weight or felt serious about changing your physique, you must appreciate the importance of your nutrition, no matter how hard you work out.

How we eat is one of the key elements to our health. While getting stronger and more flexible will help your game and how you feel immediately, changing your diet affects your body's ability to operate at the cellular level. And making the right food decisions will not only improve performance, but can also impact your long-term quality of life.

So let me ask you a serious question. Are you in this to actually make changes? Do you REALLY want to get better? If you go through the trouble of reading this book, learning how to train properly, and are actually going to put the time in at the gym, then I'll be the first to tell you that it would be pretty silly if you didn't start making some changes to your diet.

For many of you reading this book, I know you're all in, and this doesn't really apply to you. You're here to make changes, and I have a feeling you are going to go full tilt. But, I also know quite a few golfers, including many of my clients that did not start out completely committed to this piece. They didn't quite see how important the connection between their diet and training/ playing was. But I will tell you, if you start to take this part seriously, it can exponentially improve the rest of your efforts in the gym and on the course.

It's often not a lack of working out that prevents people from reaching the physical strength and aesthetics that they desire. In fact, just by reading this book, it likely tells me that getting in the gym and working hard most likely is not an issue for you. In my experience, with the golfers it's often the extra-curricular activities that hold you back: the client dinners, the golf trips, the member guest parties, the "special occasions," etc.

We all have special occasions that come up, but when an occasion crops up every weekend, I don't think you can really deem them "special" anymore. It's time to face the music and draw the line in the sand if you want to move to the next level.

I've come to realize that different people have different reasons as to why they can't get a hold on their nutrition. They generally fall into the following five categories . . .

1. You just **DON'T HAVE ENOUGH** information or know what to do.

2. You **HAVE TOO MUCH** information, and, thus, seem paralyzed, not knowing which info to trust.

3. You think you know what to do, but have **POOR INFORMATION.**

4. You know what to do, but **DON'T COMMIT** to making the change.

5. You simply **DON'T CARE!** (I can actually appreciate this group because you are at least being honest with yourself!)

This section will help the first three groups get on the right page with just a few simple principles that can't go wrong; then I need to encourage the fourth group to finally take some action and stick with it.

If you fall in the fifth group, I should scold you and tell you to wake up and realize that this section offers help about more than golf: I want to empower you so you can live a better life. But, I'm not your mother. So just take a few mental notes and come back to it when you feel ready to start making some changes. I promise I'll spare you the "I told you so" speech.

NUTRITIONAL GUIDELINES

Just to clarify (because I get the same question all of the time), before you even ask, . . .

"YES, YOU WILL HAVE TO EAT LIKE THIS
EVERY DAY FOR THE REST OF YOUR LIFE."

. . . well, almost every day.

I don't want you to think of this section as the "diet" section. I'm sure you've heard it before, but this is not a "diet." This section should be looked at as a way to start eating from here on out. You don't ever "go off of" a good eating program, you simply start making better decisions on a daily basis. Some days you'll slip and some days you'll be perfect. That's how it goes.

Different thoughts may come your way regarding how you should start making changes in your diet. On one end you have the coach with more of the drill sergeant mentality. They insist that you you must immediately log every calorie; get rid of every ounce of carbs, dairy, gluten, and fats; eat only organic, locally grown vegetables, and raise chickens in your backyard, and kill your own grass fed bull to make sure your meat is absolutely pure. This guy is a little too extreme for my taste.

On the other hand, there is the coach who always empathizes with your bad choices. He/she **"understands"** that the hotdog at the turn and five beers you had after your round were "just more convenient" and "helped you relax." This coach gives you a little encouragement and a pat on the back, hoping you will "TRY" to do better next time. (Side note: the word "TRY" is a pet peeve of mine.)

The empathetic coach's mantra sounds like, "It's OK; I know you made an effort," and you, as the client, feel less guilty and continue to repeat the same bad decisions every week.

I have found that neither of these extremes work, but a blend of both may hold the key.

As the heading implies, though, you need to realize that these changes must become a part of your routine; these guidelines are not to be turned on and off when you simply need to lose a few pounds or get ready for the beach. Optimal performance arrives when you maintain consistency over long periods of time. Thankfully, the longer the consistency, the easier it becomes.

In order to get started on this journey, I've found it very helpful to establish a few cut-and-dried guidelines around nutrition. This way, you know EXACTLY what you should do every day but don't have to break out the food journal every time you put something to your lips.

THE TIME I GOT FAT

Let me tell you another little story. This time it's about me.

OK, so I've never gotten to the point where you would've called me obese, but a time did occur in the not-too-distant past where I got a little more chunky than I care to admit.

I stopped working out; I stopped eating well, and I indulged in a certain golden beverage made of hops and barley a little more than I normally would. As I said, I live in the land of Budweiser, and a good cold beer has always been a weakness of mine.

So, as the story goes, we were doing some renovations on our house which forced us to move into my in-laws for about three months. And if that move wasn't uprooting enough, my wife was about six-months pregnant with our third child.

Over the course of these three months, I was going back and forth between residences, doing some of the work on our place myself. I had a lot of late nights, leaving the gym/office, going home to eat dinner with the family, then heading to the construction zone to get some work done.

This led to many bad late-night food and beverage choices when the evening tasks were completed. On top of that, as I mentioned, I had completely neglected my workouts given the lack of extra time in my schedule. I told myself, "it's OK, I worked hard all day, I deserve to relax a little" or "I'll get back on the fitness wagon when this is all over."

While it sounded logical and reasonable at the time, looking back, it was simply a poor decision. Anytime you decide to take a break from fundamental principles that you know are good for you, you are only doing yourself a disservice. No matter how tempting it is at the present moment.

By the end of this saga, we were blessed with a beautiful baby boy named Grant, and I found myself in desperate need to shed a little "baby fat."

At that point I decided to buckle down and hit it hard. I faced the ever-unpleasant body-fat calipers which revealed that I had climbed to almost 22% body fat (I would normally maintain the 12-15% range).

After the initial shock wore off, I knew I had to get to work. So I developed a plan of attack, enlisted a friend as an accountability partner, and even had him design some workouts for me (because, even as a fitness professional, I knew that I might be inclined to go a little easy on my own program design). Then, following the guidelines that you will see below, I got to work.

Long story long, after setting some guidelines and sticking to my plan, I shed nearly 11% of that body fat in just three months to get to a much leaner and more muscular version of myself. (If only I would have had the foresight to take some before and after pictures that I could have inserted here!)

Using the same guidelines, I promise that you too, can achieve a much higher level of personal satisfaction, you will feel better, and you will perform better on the course.

THE GUIDELINES

These are the guidelines we use at our gym with both the athletes and nonathletes. Depending on the individual, we may tweak them to some degree, but for the most part, we find that eating according to these rules will help over 90% of individuals get closer to their goals.

In the spirit of full disclosure, I did not develop this list. With the exception of #10, the rest of the list comes from the principles that nutritionist-extraordinaire Dr. John Berardi and his company, Precision Nutrition, have preached for a long time. (Check out www.precisionnutrition.com, one resource that I highly recommend; they have some of the best ideas in the business of nutrition.)

Guidelines:

1. Eat often. (Preferably every two to three hours.)

2. Eat complete, lean protein every time you eat.

3. Eat vegetables every time you eat.

4. Earn your carbs.

5. Include healthy fats in your diet.

6. Drink water, coffee, and green tea.

7. Eat as many whole foods as possible.

8. Plan on cheating.

9. Create the habit of preparation.

10. Supplement appropriately, especially around your workouts.

Depending on what your diet looks like now, just by following these guidelines, you will notice huge changes in your body composition, energy levels, sleep, and overall wellness, all of which play a major role in performance on the course. (The term "**body composition**" generally refers to an individual's body fat and lean muscle.)

Let's expand briefly on each and give a few examples so you have a little better idea of what I'm talking about.

1. **Eat Often (every two to three hours):**

   Exactly what it says. I want you to plan out having some sort of meal, or "eating opportunity," as Dr. Berardi likes to call it, frequently. This keeps you from getting famished and, surprisingly, causes your body to expend more energy (calories) as it digests the food and keeps your metabolism running at a higher rate. Your blood sugar levels will also regulate more easily since you will not undergo periods of high and low sugar intakes. This reflects on your energy levels. I will say that there are several new studies on the benefits of intermittent fasting, and it's possible benefits, but for simplicity sake, when starting out, I recommend you begin with this more frequent eating schedule.

2. **Eat Complete, Lean Protein Every Time You Eat:**

   This means that each time you have an "eating opportunity" you want to get some sort of protein in you. By "complete, lean" I mean things like chicken, fish, lean beef, elk, bison, turkey, protein powder, eggs, etc. Be creative so you don't get bored, but this is IMPERATIVE if you want to lose body fat and increase your lean muscle mass. For the record, though, **protein powder** should NOT dominate as a source of protein throughout your day. Typically, use it only in a post-workout shake or when you are in a time pinch and have no other option.

3. **Eat Vegetables Every Time You Eat:**

   And, yes, I mean EVERY TIME. If you think of veggies at breakfast as weird, I did, too. But now, you'll find a big mound of broccoli next to my eggs, or spinach and peppers mixed in my omelets. Get over it. In fact, it's not unusual to find a traditional dinner meal like chicken and veggies as a regular breakfast option at any of my clients' houses.

4. **Earn Your Carbs**:

Depending on your current eating habits, this may be the most important one for you. Especially if you eat a typical Western diet. Carbs are not "bad," as some might have you believe, but they often get eaten in huge quantities, too frequently, and very often in the wrong form (i.e., the low quality, processed, starchy kind).

Think of having to **EARN** the carbs that you eat. The only time you get to indulge in the breads, pastas, and starchy kind of carbs that we all love comes AFTER you have worked out, preferably in the two to three hours immediately post training. Otherwise, these foods can cause fluctuations in your blood sugar levels which ultimately lead to fat storage.

5. **Include HEALTHY Fats in Your Diet**:

Fats aren't the enemy. Just like carbs and proteins, our body uses and needs fats. The key lies in getting good amounts of different kinds of fats from whole food sources. This would include things like avocados, healthy raw nuts, fish oil, etc.

Be aware that the "low fat" and "no fat" versions of items that would, under normal circumstances, have fat in them. This usually means they rank as **highly processed** and, therefore, probably have added sweeteners and/or other chemicals to make them taste "better." I'll take the full fat, whole version over the processed version every time!

6. **Water, Coffee, and Green Tea**:

Think of these as your go to drinks of choice. Water, of course, ought to rank as number one on the list, and you should definitely drink it in higher quantities than the other two. But the main point here is to avoid the sugary sports drinks, the soft drinks (even the no-calorie "diet" sodas), and any fancy drink that you can't pronounce at your coffee shop.

As my personal preference, I down a large glass of lemon water in the morning before I do anything. (We even have our kids doing it every morning now. They call it their "inner bath," thanks to my buddy Shawn Stevenson over at The Model Health Show, (www.TheShawnStevensonModel.com.)

Then I'll have a cup of coffee or two. The rest of the day consists of water and maybe a green tea or coffee in the afternoon. Too much caffeine can increase your cortisol levels and other hormonal responses, which can jack up your sleep quality and cause you to store fat around the belly.

7. **Eat as Many WHOLE Foods as Possible**:

There is way too much processed food out there today, and we have all gotten used to eating it on a regular basis without a second thought. Without going into too much detail and going off on a huge tangent, the more "whole" a food is, the less processed and chemically filled it is.

Eating more whole, higher-quality foods reduces the stresses on your body and brain, allowing you to function, recover, think, react, and play better.

If you have an interest in learning more about the importance of whole foods, I have several great resources for you.

a. *The Omnivore's Dilemma* **(book) by Michael Pollan**:
   Considered the bible in learning about the food industry and the importance of understanding the **massive** difference between processed and whole/local/organic foods, this will benefit you.

b. **Precision Nutrition** (www.PrecisionNutrition):
   This site which I mentioned before has become one of my

"go to's" for all food and nutrition questions. They have some great forums and coaches there, not to mention all of their research-based resources.

c. **The Model Health Show**
(http://TheShawnStevensonModel.com/podcasts/)
Shawn Stevenson is a personal friend of mine and is at the forefront when it comes to anything nutrition, health, sleep and fitness. His podcast is full of "Master Classes" on just about every topic you want to know about.

d. **The 18STRONG Podcast** (http://18STRONG.com/podcasts/):
As I'm sure you know by now, this is my podcast. We have had so many incredible guests on the show talking about so many different topics that I will update relevant episodes in your resources page for this book (www.BogeyProofWorkout.com/resources)

8. **Plan on Cheating**:

Without this one, you'll go crazy! That's why it **has to be part of your routine**. As I mentioned before, going cold turkey, where you can never have a tasty treat again, is simply crazy, basically impossible, and only sets you up for failure. Mentally, if you know you have an opportunity each week to splurge and have a treat, some drinks or whatever, you will be less likely to go crazy and quit.

Here's the trick. You can cheat 10% of the time. Which means you should be perfect the other 90% of the time. Let's do the math:

If you eat 5 meals a day:

5 meals per day x 7 days = 35 meals
35 meals per week x 10% = 3.5 meals

If you eat 3 meals a day:

3 meals per day x 7 days = 21 meals
21 meals per week x 10% = 2.1 meals

Depending on your eating schedule, if you eat 35 meals a week, you can cheat on three to four of those meals. If you eat on a more traditional breakfast lunch, dinner schedule (21 meals a week), then you get two cheat meals.

It has been shown that there is not much of a difference in results if you eat perfectly 100% of the time or 90% of the time, so take advantage of that 10%.

A word of caution though: you have to remain honest with your meals and "cheats" as you'll often hear them referred to, or it won't work. If you skip a meal or don't meet the other require-ments, that's considered a "cheat."

9. **Create the Habit of Preparation**:

Most people get stuck here—the prep work. And I won't lie; it's not always easy, and I struggle with it, too. Born with the talent of procrastination, I struggle with thinking ahead (my wife is prob-ably nodding her head in agreement here) and planning out my weekly meals.

I've found two solutions that have worked for me and my clients.

First, try the **WEEKLY PREP SESSION**, which is my preferred method. This requires simply cooking up a large quantity of food, usually a couple kinds of meat and veggies, which I then portion out for my meals for the upcoming week. I believe the invention of crock pots came about for this purpose. "Set it and forget it!" (Possibly the greatest invention known to man)

The second option, less labor-intensive, comes at a price that's a little harder on the pockets, but is super convenient. Several of my clients use a high quality **FOOD DELIVERY SERVICE**. These have popped up everywhere, and if you can afford it, I would recommend giving one a try. They basically deliver freshly prepared, perfectly portioned, and balanced meals to your doorstep every few days.

I've seen them for between $100-$200 per week where I live, not all that bad considering the quality you get and the time you save by not having to shop for and prepare the food.

Just make sure the food is high quality, freshly prepared, and tastes good. I'm not talking about Lean Cuisine or Weight Watcher's meals here. A lot of these higher quality food services use fresh local produce and meats, which makes using and supporting these companies an awesome choice for many reasons.

10. **Supplement your nutrition appropriately, especially around your workouts**:

While whole foods should definitely be your primary source of nutrition, certain supplements exist which will improve your overall health and performance, depending on the individual and the goals. We will discuss this further in an upcoming section, so hold on to your questions.

"ANYTIME MEALS" VS. "POST-WORKOUT" MEALS

In the last section, you learned the principles that should govern your meals, including the idea that you need to get in the mindset of **EARNING** your carbs and cheat meals.

In this section, I want to clarify how to go about earning those carbs. It's really simple. This is another concept that I learned from Precision

Nutrition that has changed the way I think about eating. Start thinking of your meals as one of two types:

1. Anytime Meals
2. Post-Workout Meals

These seem pretty self-explanatory. The **"Anytime"** meals specify the way you should eat the majority of the time. These include a portion of protein, a lot of veggies, and a small amount of fats (like almonds, walnuts, avocado, etc). NO STARCHY CARBS!

The **"Post-Workout"** meals should get eaten within two to three hours after your workout (and this means a strength-training workout, not so much a cardio workout, and definitely not just a walk around the block). This consists of protein, lots of veggies, some carbs (like bread, pasta, potatoes, etc.) and very little, if any, fats.

The carbs in this situation will actually help aid in the recovery of your muscles, replenish the energy stores that you used in your workout, and help build lean muscle.

Stick to these two types of meals, and it all becomes much, much simpler.

NO SUGARS, NO GRAINS

I do feel the need to add something in this section because, the more I read and learn, the more I personally tend to sway toward this way of eating. It's pretty much as simple as the title here says: no sugars, no grains.

The premise here is that you eat the contents of the aforementioned "Anytime Meal" all the time. So I guess in this section, we could re-label it the **"All The Time Meal."**

Our bodies can become very sensitive to carbohydrates, leading to rises and falls in blood sugar (blood glucose) and insulin levels.

Processed, starchy carbs, such as breads, bagels, donuts, crackers, pretzels, etc., can have dramatic effects on these blood sugar levels which can lead to many ill effects. Some of these include:

- spikes and crashes in energy
- insulin resistance (Our body gets confused and has trouble regulating the hormonal response and production of insulin.)
- carbohydrate "spillover" which can lead to increased storage of body fat
- disruption of other hormonal balances responsible for sleep cycles and brain function.

Due to these issues, many individuals these days have made the choice to completely get rid of these foods from their diet.

At this point, my personal diet follows along relatively closely to this model, but, overall, I promote a pretty simple moderation mindset when it comes to the starchy carbs.

If you have fat-loss as your main goal, I highly recommend looking at this way of eating (higher protein, higher in good fats, very low in carbs). I have used it personally and with many clients to shed quite a bit of body fat in a relatively short period of time—all the while, feeling great and without complications.

One of my favorite sources for more information on this comes from a well known fitness expert by the name of Vinnie Tortorich. He has a great podcast on iTunes, "The Angriest Trainer Podcast," which you can find on his website: http://VinnieTortorich.com/

"PERI-WORKOUT" NUTRITION

"Peri" simply means "around" or "surrounding." Therefore, "peri-workout nutrition" refers to the food and supplements that you eat before, during, and after your workouts.

We'll keep this pretty simple. Many different supplements and/or foods exist that you can take/eat before, after, and during workouts, many of which you might find very effective in assisting fat-loss and lean muscle development. However, for the scope of this book, I want simply to focus on the basics and not confuse you more by giving you too much information.

Before the Workout

You want to make sure that you have some fuel in your body before working out. By this, I mean make sure you have eaten within a couple of hours before your workout.

Let me tell you a story. I had a client a couple of years ago, in his early 30's, a highly competitive amateur golfer, and in very good shape. His workouts were normally very challenging, but he was always up to the task—with the exception of this one day.

His workout was at 7 a.m. He showed up a little bit tardy. He woke up a bit late that day and had rushed to the gym. After going through his warm-up, we got into our initial exercises. I had decided to incorporate some bike sprints that day, and guess what? After the second round of sprints, he asked to go to the restroom. After about five minutes, another gym member came up to me and said, "Hey, Jeff, you might want to go check on your guy. He is lying on the locker-room floor!"

He ended up being fine, but he got a little queasy, lightheaded, and wanted to throw up. And what do you think the first question I asked was? "Did you eat anything today?" Of course, he hadn't. So we got him some water and something to put in his stomach. I then sent him on his way for the day because there was no way we would make any progress at that point.

There have been more than a handful of times I've had someone get dizzy, nauseous, and have to sit down because they didn't feel well. And 99% of the time, they had not eaten that morning before coming to the gym. Their body didn't have anything on which to fuel itself for energy, so it went into shutdown mode. The good news, though, is that once you learn the lesson the hard way, you usually don't forget to fuel up before a workout ever again.

Within two hours or so before your workout, get some sort of a meal in you. The closer you get to the workout, the less dense you want it to be. Proteins and fats are pretty dense substances and will sit in your stomach, so give them some time to settle.

If you have to hurry, something with a little more carbs will suit because it will give your body something to work with and won't sit in your stomach like a rock. You will likely burn it up as energy, so it won't hurt you from the standpoint of being a carb. Preferably though, you should schedule one of your anytime meals properly before training.

During the Workout

While you work out, I recommend staying hydrated simply with water or a BCAA (Branch Chain Amino Acid) drink. BCAA's basically prevent your body from breaking down muscle tissue to use as energy during and after your workouts. BCAA's can also help in preventing soreness and increasing your body's ability to burn fat.

Several good BCAA products have hit the market which come in either a powder form which you can mix in your water or in a capsule form that you simply take during your workouts between sets.

This may be getting a little too involved for the novice trainee, so your best bet is to start with just water and learn more about BCAA's to see if they seem right for you. Whatever you do, just please stay away from the sugar-laden, artificial-sweetener-laced, crappy sports drinks.

A couple of companies that produce high quality BCAA products are Biosteel, EXOS, Controlled Labs, and Champion Nutrition to name a few.

After the Workout

Without hesitation, I want you to follow this advice: drink a post-workout shake. And if you can't, for whatever reason, then make sure you eat within one hour after your workout.

This advice is key to your body recovering properly and your ability to gain lean muscle and strength. Within a short period of time after your workout, your body goes into a "catabolic state."

"Catabolic" means your body starts breaking down tissue (including muscle) to repair itself, which is exactly the opposite of what you want it to given the fact that you are working out. In order to promote an "anabolic" or growing state, we must feed it the right nutrition and get it into the system quickly to help prevent muscle breakdown. By drinking a post workout shake (which should include protein, some carbs, and BCAA's), you can help slow down and even prevent some of the catabolic effects of the workout.

Some recommendations for companies that produce high quality post workout shakes include: Biosteel, Champion Nutrition, EXOS, and Designs for Health.

ON COURSE NUTRITION

While this technically doesn't fall into the category of "workout nutrition," being that this is a book for golfers, I think it's important to address what you are fueling yourself with on the course.

You can make all the changes in the gym and at home, but if you're not ready and fueled when you step on the tee box, you're body won't be able to perform to it's potential. Along the same lines, especially if you are playing consecutive days or multiple rounds in a day, we need to take a look at what you're eating before and after.

In many ways, your round of golf is kind of like your workout. It's a physical activity where you are draining your energy stores. It just happens to be for a longer period of time and isn't quite as dense in volume or intensity as a workout would be.

Using the same line of thinking though, let's look at 3 specific time periods:

1. Pre-Round
2. In-Round
3. Post-Round

Pre-Round Nutrition

Before a round of golf, our main focus is to prepare our body and mind for the round. So we want to improve and maintain focus, brain function, and energy levels. To do this, I suggest you emphasize 3 sources of fuel:

- lean meats
- vegetables/low glycemic fruits
- good fats (I suggest coconut oil)

The **lean meats** provide protein that reduces hunger and boosts brain function. As an added long-term benefit, lean meat is associated with less body fat, more muscle mass, and faster recovery from soft tissue injuries.

The **vegetables and low glycemic fruit** promote a steadier rise in blood sugar and insulin levels for sustained energy. Higher glycemic foods can spike and crash blood sugar levels, leaving you tired and lethargic.

The **good fats**, specifically the coconut oil, are beneficial because they are a Medium Chain Triglyceride (MCT) oil. Because it is not a long chain fatty acid, storing coconut oil as body fat is unlikely, thus leaving it readily available for energy use. It is also antiviral, antibacterial, and antifungal. Coconut oil boosts the immune system and thyroid and is very easily digestible. A quick warning here though . . .

Avoid all hydrogenated coconut oil!

In-Round Nutrition

During your round, your goal is simple: Stay focused on the round.

The best way to do this is by staying hydrated, maintaining your energy level, and keeping your brain sharp. In order to achieve these goals, I recommend having a couple of things with you during your round.

- Electrolytes
- Essential Amino Acids (EAA)/ Branched Chain Amino Acids (BCAA)
- Nuts
- Jerky

These are my go to snacks for the course.

The **electrolytes** and **EAA/BCAA's** can often be found together in a powder form that you simply mix with water in a shaker bottle. There are several brands that have become popular in the golf world. Most of your reputable supplement companies will have a product that you can use for this purpose. (See the next section on supplements before just picking any brand.)

I like to bring some form of **mixed raw nuts** on the course as well. They are easy to pack up and travel with and are a great low glycemic energy source. Nuts won't spike your blood sugar. Notice that I specified that they be RAW. When nuts are roasted, they lose the healthy properties that provide the benefits of increased mental function and clarity.

Also, in case you don't already know this, peanuts are not really nuts. They are legumes. Therefore, these would not be on my ideal list. My personal preference is almonds, cashews, macadamia nuts, and/or walnuts.

And lastly, I love **jerky**, mainly because it's just so freaking delicious! But from the nutrition side, jerky is a great protein source that, once again, is easy to travel with. I also love it because it doesn't need to be refrigerated, it's not greasy, and can be consumed easily while walking.

When you are shopping for all of these items, I encourage you to look for the purest brands possible. The more natural, the better. One easy way to tell is to look at the list of ingredients. As a general rule of thumb, look for the products that have fewer ingredients overall and the majority of the ingredients should be real foods that you can pronounce the name of. I have seen bags of beef jerky with over 100 ingredients vs others that have closer to 5.

Post-Round Nutrition

The goal of the post round nutrition is simply to provide a speedy recovery for your next round.

Now, I understand that often a post round snack comes in a frosty mug, but we are talking ideals here. If you are really wanting to maximize your recovery, these little things can give you that extra edge.

My suggestion here would be to have a whey protein shake ready to go after your round. It's easily digestible and provides the amino acids for tissue building and recovery. Plus the BCAA's in the shake can help prevent soreness in the muscles.

This is super easy to do, too. All you have to do is put a couple scoops of protein powder in a shaker bottle before your round and keep it in your bag or car. Then, when you finish your round, just add some water to your shaker, and, BOOM, there you go.

If you do all of these the next couple of times you play, and you stay away from the snack bar at the turn, I promise you will notice more energy and stamina at the end of your round.

In the next section we'll get into a little more detail about the whole world of supplements, including what is actually worth taking, and whether you are even ready to start thinking about it.

SUPPLEMENTS

Before delving into this topic, this seems like an appropriate place to make it very clear that **I am not a nutritionist or dietitian** and that I simply want to provide you with material that I have learned over the years. I am in no way prescribing a diet and supplementation plan for you. As always, consult a proper medical professional if you want specific advice as to what would constitute the right food and supplement program for you.

As mentioned before, whole foods set the gold standard when it comes to nutrition, but in today's society, the abundance of supplements available warrants a discussion revolving around some important factors to consider before heading to the vitamin shop.

True, some supplements may act in a very helpful way in achieving your highest fitness goals and getting you closer to "**optimal nutrition**" (a very subjective term). But for the most part, you really should focus on getting the eating part down first, then worry about any supplementation after that. Too many people worry about what vitamins and shakes they should take, but pay no attention to what they put on their plates (or pull out of the fast-food bag) every day.

Also, before I go into a little detail about a few different supplements, another issue arises that I must first address: **the quality of the supplements**. If you think a vitamin is a vitamin and every fish-oil pill is the same, then please pay attention.

At the time I am writing this book, the supplement world is very poorly regulated. Good products exist, but bad—if not harmful—products get offered on the shelves and online, too, depending on the brands you choose. If the raw materials used in the products do not start out good, clean, and healthy; if the manufacturing facility hasn't been cleaned sufficiently every day; or the company makes multiple products on the same equipment, you have a chance of obtaining supplements contaminated with undesirable things such as metals, allergens, and other substances that you would rather not put in your body.

It is important to do your homework first. Find a reputable company that has a good track record. Some companies—like NSF, Consumer Labs, Informed Choice, and a few others—are third-party testing companies with the sole purpose of evaluating supplements for safety and regulation.

Look for the stamp of approval from one of these companies, and you can at least feel reassured that what the label says is what is actually in the bottle. If you want to know the brands that I use and what we use with our athletes at our gym, feel free to contact me and/or check our resources page at www.BogeyProofWorkout.com/resources.

What Should I Be Taking?

I generally encourage my clients to put their supplements in a hierarchical order of what is most beneficial and cost-effective. The order that I generally recommend follows here:

- whole foods (follow the guidelines described earlier)
- fish oil
- multivitamins
- post-workout shake
- BCAA mix or capsules during workout

As another word of warning, I encourage all of my clients to consult their physicians regarding the use of supplements, especially if they are currently taking any medication. I expect you to do the same. Be smart about what you put in your body, no matter who tells you to do so. You should always be an informed consumer!

Regarding the hierarchical order mentioned above, what I mean here is that, first, you should focus on your whole food intake and get it on track with the principles we talked about above. I am a realist, and I know that option is not always possible, but many times it is simply overlooked.

After that, I think you should take a look at your finances and your level of dedication and realistic compliance. If you can afford one extra supplement, go with fish oil. If you can afford two, then also get the multi. And so on. If money doesn't concern you and you are committed to actually using these supplements, then go ahead and start using all of them.

Or better yet, I suggest you go get your blood tested and get a complete workup for an objective look at what is really right for you. (Note: I am not talking about a simple test that your general practitioner does. I am talking about a full micro-nutrient blood test, which can be performed by a qualified practitioner.)

Just don't fall into the "Supplement Snowball Effect" where you start relying more on the pills and powders to provide your nutrition than the real food you eat.

Nothing can replace what whole foods do for you. The readers who understand this will more likely reach their lean muscle and fat loss goals; the ones who don't will simply stay fat or get fat.

Now I'll provide you with the quick and dirty on each of these supplements. Specific dosages of each of these may differ for each individual, based on size, nutritional deficits, and brands of products. Therefore, I will not give you any specifics in regards to dosages for each one.

As mentioned before, smarter people than I can give you this advice. I'm not a nutritionist, dietician, or doctor, and I don't pretend to be an authority on nutrition. With that said, I will throw in a few fancy words surrounded mainly by layman's terms, which is the only way I can understand it all.

Fish Oil

Fish oils are Omega 3 Essential Fatty Acids (EFA's), which the body cannot produce on it's own. Specifically, you will find EPA and DHA are the EFA's in fish oil. These Omega 3's have been linked to many health benefits, including:

- reduction of general inflammation in the body
- reduction of joint inflammation
- improvement of cardiovascular function
- improvement of cognition, brain development, and nervous system function (especially in a developing fetus)
- improvement in immunity
- ignition of the fat-burning genes (lipolysis)
- extinguishing of the fat-storage genes (lipogenesis)

You can take fish oil in either capsule or liquid form. I personally take it in the liquid form. I find it easier to ingest higher quantities in the liquid form, and it also costs less (at least in my experience).

Multivitamin

I like to think of the multivitamin as the security blanket. Even when you do your best to eat right and consume mainly whole foods, good proteins, lots of veggies, etc., it is still likely that holes exist in your nutritional profile. The multivitamin helps to fill those holes by providing a broad spectrum of the most important vitamins and minerals.

While some may need this more than others based on their diet, I recommend that everyone take a multi as more of a security measure than an "end all and be all" wonder pill.

*Again, this should be a **pharmaceutical grade** product, not your generic or even popular brand from the nearest drug store.*

Post-Workout Shake

The post-workout shake is also known as a recovery shake. Basically, the idea is that, when you work out, you break down your body and muscle tissue. Your body uses up the stored energy in order to perform your lifts and then begins to go to other sources (your muscles, proteins, etc.) to get more energy, either to finish your workout or to begin the recovery process.

If you do not adequately replenish your body with the proper nutrients within the next 45 minutes or so, your body will lack the ability to recover properly.

There are differing philosophies as to what makes the ideal post-workout shake, but, as a general rule-of-thumb, **if your goal is to build lean muscle**, your shake should be fairly high in protein and contain nearly twice the amount of carbs as proteins. In this short window after your workout, your body's spike in insulin allows these carbs to be utilized in the repair process of the muscles. (I generally would recommend this to a client if he ranks at or below the 10% bodyfat range).

If your goal is to burn fat, you might simply want to use a high quality protein shake that has low sugars and carbs since your main goal is simply to burn energy. While increasing muscle mass may also be a goal, you have to decide which is more important, the loss of fat or the building of mass.

If you are on more of a "fat-adapted" diet, then the "low-to-no" carb and sugar option is what you want. (A "fat-adapted" diet falls in line with the "No Sugars, No Grains" model we talked about earlier. We will not cover the physiological details in this book, but it is definitely something about which I suggest you educate yourself to see if it might be right for you).

Ultimately, you may find that a certain combination works better for you. The only real way to find out comes from trial and error. Use one type of post-workout shake for a month and document your result (e.g., weight and body fat %). Then try a different ratio of carbs/proteins the next month and compare your records.

BCAAs (Branched Chain Amino Acids)

These are the building blocks of protein. They are also burned for energy during exercise. If we have adequate amounts of BCAA's in our diet and, specifically, at the time of exercise, the BCAA's help prevent the break-down of muscle protein during and after the workouts.

In short, by using a peri-workout drink with a BCAA mixture or BCAA capsules, you will likely have more energy and less protein breakdown from your workout, both of which contribute to gains in strength and muscle.

DRAW THE LINE IN THE SAND

Now we arrive at the time to put some of this into action. As your first step you must simply make a decision that you plan to change your habits. You don't have to start with all of them. That would be crazy, and **you will fail** if you try that approach.

I've seen it too many times. Someone jumps in, goes all out for a week, a month, maybe even a couple of months. But soon enough, it gets to him, and he says "forget it." Then gives up. That's not what I want to see.

I want to see you succeed at this, and, as the best way to do that, you should pick one thing from above and commit to doing it 90% of the time for the next two weeks. If you want to do some of the other stuff, by all means, go for it, but commit to just one thing. I'll even make a suggestion.

If you don't usually eat breakfast or your breakfast is often a carbohydrate-laden feast like cereal, bagels, oatmeal, toast, etc., just commit to eating an **"Anytime Meal"** for breakfast every day. That would be something like eggs, a veggie, and a handful of nuts.

If you can do that 90% of the time for the next two to four weeks, you'll not only feel better, but it won't seem so hard anymore. At that point, you can add in another commitment because the first one has now become part of your routine.

As these start adding up, I guarantee you'll notice some big changes in the way you look, feel, and play.

BOGEY-PROOF ACTION TIPS FOR EXCELLENT NUTRITION STRATEGIES

- Weigh yourself and get your body fat checked by a professional.
- Determine your nutrition goals. Do you want to lose fat, gain muscle, etc.? Write them down.
- Pick one commitment regarding a diet change and stick to it for at least two weeks.
- Progressively increase your adherence to the ten guidelines from this chapter.
- Once you're crushing the eating guidelines, look into the supplements that suit you and your goals best.

Podcasts? Cheat sheet of the 10 guidelines?
Find these and more at BogeyProofWorkout.com/resources.

#4
QUALITY OF EXECUTION

I f you walk into your average commercial gym anywhere in America, I guarantee what goes on in there looks a lot different from what you see when you walk into a high-quality sports performance/training facility.

Often, the commercial gym simply supports "contained chaos," where there is little rhyme or reason to the exercises performed, and in many cases you'll find a definite lack of regard for quality of movement, posture, form, tempo, and proper program design.

I assume you no longer want to be a part of this demographic, and I congratulate you on that decision.

Now the time has come for you to actually put some hours and effort into preparing your workouts, learning how to perform the exercises properly, and achieving some actual results. Your days of going to the gym just to say you "went to the gym" are over.

In this section, I will show you how to work out with a purpose. Once you get it in your head that your workouts need structure, a well thought out plan, a schedule, and that you have to perform them deliberately and intensely, you're looking at a **game changer** in your road to improvement.

I'll be the first to admit that, when I first started working out and, unfortunately, for some of my clients in the beginning of my career, I had no idea how to design a decent program. So don't feel bad if you feel the same way.

It has taken years of reading, learning, making mistakes, and working with some great coaches (my current business partner and strength coaches at my facility being some of my biggest mentors) to get to the point where I am today. And, no surprise, two years from today, when I look back, it'll seem like I barely knew anything even now. That's just how it goes. That's how we know we are growing and getting better.

But, thankfully, I have learned a lot, and gone are the days of throwing together a few exercises on a sheet of paper right before my workout—or, even worse, just minutes before my client walks in the door for their workout. If you've ever found yourself wandering around the gym, trying to figure out what exercises you wanted to do that day, rest assured, I've been there, too, but I'm going to show you a better way.

I'll give you a suggestion. If you ever go to the gym and you don't have a program to follow, I DO NOT want you to walk around for ten minutes, trying to decide what you feel like doing that day. Instead of wasting that hour getting nothing done, what you should do is this:

- Do 20 minutes of sprint intervals on the bike or treadmill and then leave the gym.
- Go home or somewhere quiet.
- Take 20 minutes and write out a program that you can commit to for the next 4-6 weeks. (If you need a template for this, you can find one at www.BogeyProofWorkout.com/resources.)

- Go back to the gym the next day and start your program.
- Work your tail off for four weeks and then repeat the process with a new program.
- Enjoy your new-found strength, flexibility, energy, and golf game!

EVERY EXERCISE HAS A PURPOSE

We all make mistakes, and I can't claim immunity on this one. Unfortunately, in the not so distant past, I, too, plead guilty of simply making stuff up on the fly for my own workouts. Even worse, the content of the client programs that I created were at times based more on what I knew would make the clients happy, not what would really get them to a desired short- or long-term goal.

I wanted them to **feel** as though they got a good workout. I often didn't have a structured, well thought-out program that had a vision as to the progression of how I would get them to their goal.

Fortunately for you, I learned from these mistakes. I don't want you to continue on the same path. You work out for a reason and, hopefully, have some sort of goal in mind, either physically or golf-related. It only makes sense that every element of your program should focus on achieving those goals.

Every exercise that you put in a workout should have a specific purpose. This may sound super obvious, but, believe me, after working in a gym, you observe some silly and questionable exercises performed by the members and, even worse, suggested by the trainers.

When coming up with exercises, you don't have to over complicate it, either. I simply encourage you to ask yourself a few questions:

- **Why am I putting this exercise in my program?**

- **Can I perform this exercise properly with good form and full range of motion?**

- **Does the exercise and how I am executing it (reps, sets, tempo) get me closer to my goal of becoming. . . (stronger, more balanced, leaner, bigger, more flexible, etc.)?**

- **Is this truly an effective exercise for this workout, or could I find a more effective one?**

If you can't answer these questions positively, then you may want to rethink the contents of your program. But, if you feel like the exercises you've chosen fit well for your goals and you can perform them properly, by all means, get ready to crush it!

MOVEMENT FIRST

Sometimes it pains me to watch people do certain exercises. One sticks out most in my head: **the squat**. The squat is one of the greatest and most fundamental exercises that you can do. I don't care if it's with a bar, dumbbells, or just body weight, I believe it is an exercise that everyone of us should strive to perform well.

I realize that everyone in the world cannot do this and many of us have limitations that physically won't allow a full range squat. Some of those limitations are correctable and some are not. With that being said, I have seen some really bad squats.

In many of these cases (and this goes for a lot of other exercises that are commonly performed incorrectly), I believe the individual most likely has never been taught or shown how to squat properly, and therefore may be able to achieve this goal purely with better instruction and a solid visual model.

In other cases, many individuals don't focus or better yet, even pay attention to the motion enough to discern the fact that they are doing it incorrectly.

And, lastly, many individuals just don't have the **mobility** or **stability** to do it right.

This brings me to my point. You may not have the proper motion to do an exercise correctly. Odds are you cannot perform quite a few exercises properly due to restrictions in your body.

If you find this is the case, **we must work on fixing that issue before adding weight to certain exercises in your program**.

All too often I see individuals trying to perform exercises with loads of weight that they could not do correctly even if they didn't use any weight at all! What do you think will happen if you take a bad movement, add weight to it, and do it a bunch of times? You have an almost guaranteed **recipe for injury**.

As professor Pavel Kolar, one of the most popular names in the world of human development and rehabilitation recently explained it to me (I'm paraphrasing here). . .

"[It's like a drip of water over time. Initially it doesn't appear to have any effect, but over given enough duration it can do enough damage to create a canyon]."

This again reiterates the point that you have to do the simple exercise correctly before you can start packing on the weights. If you see a restriction in your motion, either start working on ways to fix it or seek out a professional who can help you figure out what you need to do to attack that problem.

If the motion is messed up in the gym, you better believe that it will likely have an effect on your golf game.

POSTURE IS KEY

Your golf swing revolves around posture. I'll go even further and say that your overall health and quality of life, in many ways, revolves around your posture.

Look at the guys on tour today and you will notice more than ever the amount of players who set up to the ball with perfect posture.

Unfortunately for the majority of us, 90% of our day is dominated by situations that encourage us to sit, stand or walk with poor posture. As much time as our generation spends in a forward, rounded-shoulder position at our desks, in the car, on the couch, and sleeping in the fetal position, it's almost surprising to me that we have not regressed to walking on all fours again.

Due to all of this postural stress that we put on our bodies, the importance grows even more than ever that you become aware of how you move in your workouts. By emphasizing the proper positioning of the shoulders, head, and spine in all of the movements that you perform, you reinforce the good habits and prevent permanent changes that lead to poor posture and injury.

Initially, this may prove hard to do consistently. But, the more you work on executing every move perfectly with the head, spine, feet, etc., in what we call "neutral alignment," you educate your body to move more efficiently, quickly, and more powerfully.

Our body basically runs on electricity in the form of impulses sent from the brain to the body and vice versa. When you have your body properly aligned, especially in regards to the spine, you allow your nerves to conduct those impulses faster and more efficiently. I encourage you to consider this as a very important component in your golf swing, which is just a sequence of very fast stresses placed on the body.

Not only is it the nerves that are affected, but if our spine is out of alignment (out of neutral position) it restricts movement in many areas of the body.

Let's look at the thoracic spine for instance. We are meant to rotate primarily from this area, the mid-upper back. But if your spine is hunched forward, it will drastically reduce your rotation.

Let me show you what I mean. Try this right now. Sit up as tall as you can. Cross your arms in front of your chest so your hands are on your shoulders. Now I want you to start rotating back and forth from the right to the left. Pay attention to how much motion you have. Also note what your abdominals feel like. There should be some stretching and a little tension as you go back and forth.

Now I want you to slouch. Same position with the hands and arms, but let your shoulders round, let your head jut forward, and hunch your upper back. Now try to rotate.

What do you notice? There is a significant reduction in how far you can rotate. How do your abs feel? Do they feel engaged and powerful, or do they feel doughy, relaxed, and sloppy? I'm guessing the latter.

Think about the effect that has on your golf swing. Simply changing your posture to a more advantageous position will result in a massive improvement in your ability to transfer power from your lower body out to the clubhead.

As a great follow up to this section, I would encourage you to listen to an interview I did with Brian Bradley from Egoscue University on the podcast. You can go to the link HERE, or you can download it in the resources section at www.BogeyProofWorkout.com/Resources

TYPES OF MUSCLE CONTRACTIONS AND MUSCLE FIBERS

Before we go to the next section and discuss one of the most overlooked and underutilized fundamentals in strength training—**the tempo**—we have to talk a little about how the body works: more specifically, how our muscles work.

I'm going to warn you right now. This section gets a little technical, and if you're not a nerd for this stuff like me, it might get a bit boring. But, please know that I put this in here for a reason. If you can understand this section (which really isn't all that bad) you will have a much better understanding why the next section is so important. So please bear with me.

OK, so here we go. Muscle contractions can be described in three different types:

1. **Concentric**—shortening of the muscle
2. **Eccentric**—lengthening of the muscle
3. **Isometric**—contraction while maintaining the same length.

As a familiar example, let's use the **bench-press** exercise to explain the difference between the three.

When performing the bench press, you first lift the bar off the rack and then lower it to your chest. The lowering of the bar is the **eccentric phase,** during which the chest muscles are lengthening as you bring the weight down.

As you transition to the lifting/pressing portion of the exercise, this is known as the **concentric phase**, during which the muscles shorten. This shortening of the muscles allows you to push the weight upward.

If at any time during the exercise, you would stop and hold a position, we would consider that an **isometric phase**. During an isometric phase, your muscles generate tension, but they do not move; thus, they do not shorten or lengthen at that given time.

Another way I like to describe it to my clients is that during the eccentric phase of a free-weight exercise, gravity helps the weight move. During the concentric phase, you fight gravity to move the weight in the other direction, against the earth's force.

What is interesting about the different types of contraction is that there is a descending strength curve between the three. Your eccentric strength ranks as the strongest; isometric strength comes next in line, and your concentric strength ranks as the weakest of the three.

Eccentric ⇨ Isometric ⇨ Concentric

This might seem confusing, but when you think about it, imagine yourself on the bench press. If I loaded up the weight, you would find it easier to slowly lower it to your chest than you would to hold it up isometrically with your elbows slightly bent.

But, it would be easier to hold the weight up than if we started the weight at the bottom and I told you to push it up, right?

Thus, you can lower more weight than you can hold, and you can hold more weight than you can lift.

IT'S ALL ABOUT THE TEMPO

Now that we have addressed the different types of muscle contractions and you understand the difference between an eccentric, isometric, and concentric contraction, we can discuss what I feel stands as the most unappreciated fundamental of a workout: the **tempo**.

Again, stay with me here while we get a bit technical. Read through this section a couple of times if it doesn't make sense the first time. It will eventually, I promise. If my 75+ year old client with no previous training background can get it, I'm confident that you will too.

I have a question for you. Do you want to just get through your workout, or do you want to actually get something out of your workout?

Have you ever seen the guy in the gym doing biceps curls or triceps press-downs at breakneck speed? It looks more like he is running a jackhammer as opposed to training. Don't be that guy. We make fun of that guy. In fact, we don't tolerate that guy in our gym.

The speed at which you perform your exercises should remain thought-out and deliberate. And guess what: I bet you do most of your tempos backwards.

If you subscribe to the same thought process as 90% of the general public, you concentrate your efforts in your lifts on raising the bar/dumbbell (the **concentric phase**).

Those who know the importance of the "time-under-tension" principle focus their efforts more on the descent of the weight, or the **eccentric phase**, than the **concentric phase**. Why? Because this is where more time is spent under tension, and the muscles can handle more load.

The concentric phase is important, but it is a much faster movement; therefore, the muscles are not stressed for as significant a period of time. When the muscle comes under stress, we are challenging the tissue to its fullest, which, in the long run, makes it bigger and stronger.

For this reason, we teach every client at our facility to stay very aware of the tempo of each exercise. Sometimes we will make the eccentric phase of the lift longer or shorter, depending on the exercise and our motive for the exercise (i.e., strength, power, speed, endurance, building mass, fat loss, etc.). I'll give you a few examples in just a bit.

Does this sound confusing? Or do you think it seems a little "over-the-top" specific? I did, too, when I first saw someone write out the tempo of their exercises for a client. But I was wrong. This may be the single most important thing I have learned and begun applying to my programs in the past five years.

This simple technique (and I will show you how to properly write the tempo on a program) has completely changed the way I work out. Not only has it opened my eyes about my personal strength and fitness routines, but, now that I know this secret, I also would **NEVER** give my clients a program without specifying the tempo on each exercise. It's that important.

I'll show you partial examples of what part of a program can look like. The following tables are all taken from real programs that have been written at our facility over the years. While the layout of each is a little different, the fundamentals are all similar.

A1-Quads	W	Set/R	Rep	Tempo	Weight
	1	4/45s	6-8	3010	
	2	4/45s	6-8	3010	
	3	4/45s	6-8	3010	
	4	4/45s	6-8	3010	
	5	4/45s	6-8	3010	
	6	4/45s	6-8	3010	
	Note		Barbell squat		

Figure 1

A) BARBELL DEADLIFT

Wk	S x R	Tempo	Rest		s1	s2	s3	s4	s5	s6
1	6X6	3010	90	weight						
				reps						
2	6X6	3010	90	weight						
				reps						
3	6X6	3010	90	weight						
				reps						
4	6X6	3010	90	weight						
				reps						

Figure 2

DAY 2 - LOWER BODY 1

ORDER	EXERCISE	SETS	REPS	REST	TEMPO
A1	Squat Heels Elevated	5	8,7,6,5,4	90	3110
A2	Toes Neutral & Dorsi/Plantarflexed Leg Curl	5	8,7,6,5,4	90	4010
B1	DB Drop Lunges	3	8	75	20X0
B2	Snatch Grip Romanian DL	3	8	75	3010
C	Seated Calf Raise	3	12>10>8	60	1010

Figure 3

You will notice the tempo next to each exercise. It consists of four numbers. In Figure 1 and Figure 2, the tempo numbers are all 3-0-1-0. These numbers represent time in seconds.

When reading a tempo, the first number always goes with the **eccentric phase** (in this case "3"). The second number stands for the transition from the eccentric phase to the concentric phase. So in our example of the bench press, this would represent the amount of time taken between the end of the lowering phase and the start of the pressing phase. The "0" in this example means that no pause exists between the eccentric and concentric phase.

The third number in the sequence ("1") indicates that the concentric phase should take one second to complete. And the final number ("0") shows that there is no pause at the top of the motion before starting into the next rep.

To help, I have here two more examples with explanations:

3–0–1–1	4–1–1–0
3—Eccentric 3 sec	**4**—Eccentric 4 sec
0—Pause 0 sec	**1**—Pause 1 sec
1—Concentric 1 sec	**1**—Concentric 1 sec
1—Pause 1 sec	**0**—Pause 0 sec

YOU DON'T HAVE TO PUKE

A lot of "high intensity," fast-moving, *work-till-you-pass-out* types of programs get promoted in the fitness world these days. Along with these programs comes the mentality that if you are not close to fainting or grabbing a bucket to throw up, then you didn't put in enough effort.

Yes, I believe you should give it everything you have in the gym, and, yes, sometimes I like to see a client gassed to near the breaking point, but only when it serves a purpose. As a golfer, there never comes a time in your game where the physiological stresses would come even close to that of, say, a UFC fighter, so why should you train like one?

In golf, you have to stand strong, flexible, powerful, balanced, and consistent. Ideally, that involves staying lean and muscular, too, but, as for having the lung capacity of a boxer, I see it as just not necessary.

Spend your time and effort in better ways in other areas.

Again, focus mainly on form, tempo, and, most importantly, injury prevention. It's very difficult to concentrate on these three things if you exhaust yourself in your workout. Also, we want to get the most bang for our buck with every lift or movement that you do in the gym. For this, you need adequate rest-breaks between sets and a good balance of the right exercises.

You will notice in the chart below that we also designate the amount of rest that is to be included for each set and exercise.

DAY 2 - LOWER BODY 1

ORDER	EXERCISE	SETS	REPS	REST	TEMPO
A1	Squat Heels Elevated	5	8,7,6,5,4	90	3110
A2	Toes Neutral & Dorsi/Plantarflexed Leg Curl	5	8,7,6,5,4	90	4010
B1	DB Drop Lunges	3	8	75	20X0
B2	Snatch Grip Romanian DL	3	8	75	3010
C	Seated Calf Raise	3	12>10>8	60	1010

You should determine your rest breaks by the intensity (how much weight) and volume (how many sets and reps you do). Generally, if you do fewer reps, you will do more sets,have longer rest breaks, and lift heavier weight. These workouts are geared more toward **strength- or power-development**.

The opposite would be the case for higher reps. Generally, you should do fewer sets and use lighter weights with shorter rest breaks. These are usually geared more toward **fat-loss and endurance**. And in between these come reps and tempos for **increasing muscle-mass (hypertrophy)**.

Below is a chart with some very basic guidelines just to get you started.

Type	#Reps	Weight	Rest
Fat Loss	10-20	Light	15-45 sec
Hypertrophy	8-12	Mid Range	45-90 sec
Strength	5-8	Heavy	60-120 sec
Power	3-5	Heavy	90-180 sec

Plenty of ways exist to incorporate sprints and high intensity intervals into a workout or to use them on opposite days from strength training in order to burn fat and increase cardiovascular conditioning, but I would encourage you to stay smart when combining them. Ask yourself,

"Am I able to perform these exercises with complete focus and intensity, or is the exhaustion causing me to sacrifice the quality of my other exercises?"

In a book by strength-coach Christian Thibaudeau I first came across the philosophy that "you know you performed a good set when you are slightly out of breath after finishing." That's what I recommend in your **strength** exercises.

Each set should challenge you, given the number of reps that have been chosen. If you don't struggle a little to get the last rep, you may want to add a little weight or make it harder to some degree.

My point here is that you don't measure the success of a workout necessarily by the amount of sweat on your shirt or if you have to lie on the ground, sucking wind at the end. Unfortunately, many trainers, trainees, and coaches use that as the ultimate gauge of their workouts. Any trainer in the world can make you puke if that's what you want, but does that make you a better golfer? I, personally, do not believe so.

A better way to judge your workout might be by asking the following questions:

- **Was I stronger this session than last week?**
- **Was my form perfect during every exercise?**
- **Did I push myself on every set or during every sprint?**
- **Am I improving in my weak or inflexible areas?**

If you can answer yes to these questions, then I would say you're working hard, with a purpose, and are seeing very positive progress.

BOGEY-PROOF ACTION TIPS FOR HIGHER QUALITY EXECUTION

- Pick high-quality exercises in line with the objectives of your program which will reduce your imbalances and weaknesses.
- Assess whether you can **move** through the complete motion of the exercise before adding weight. If not, work on correcting the movement first.
- Perform every rep with perfect posture to ensure that you ingrain proper movement patterns.
- Give each exercise a designated tempo and emphasize the **eccentric** contraction to maximize your strength gains.
- Measure the quality of your workout by
  - how well you performed the exercises
  - how much improvement you have made
  - how hard you pushed during each set
  - but **NOT** by how much you sweat or if you threw up!

Find these tips and more at BogeyProofWorkout.com/resources.

#5
A WILLINGNESS TO CHALLENGE YOURSELF

With the introduction of "golf-fitness" over the past decade or so, some really great fitness professionals and organizations have received notoriety for their contributions to the game. It's incredible to see the athleticism and dedication to fitness that so many of the up-and-coming golfers exhibit.

Even your average "country clubber" now realizes that working out can have an impact on his golf game. This has created an entire industry of fitness equipment, gadgets, and, most exciting of all, **employment for guys like me!** So, I remain completely grateful for the surge of golfers into the gym.

But with popularity come misconceptions, misinformation, and, sometimes, bad judgment.

It has long been said that golfers shouldn't lift weights for fear of getting too big and inflexible. While that theory seems to be dying to some extent as we see guys like Rory McIlroy working out harder than ever in the gym, and the physique of guys like Jason Day increasing on the links, the majority of the golf world still seems a little confused as to what works in the gym and what doesn't.

"BUT THAT DOESN'T LOOK LIKE A GOLF SWING"

I'll let you in on a little secret. I kind of hate the term "golf-fitness." I know that may seem hypocritical since I make my living as a "golf-fitness professional," but I feel that the term creates a misconception of what I and many excellent coaches do with our golfers. It's not just about making an exercise look or feel like a golf swing.

Golf, just like any other sport, relies on the fact that the stronger, faster, more flexible, powerful, and consistent you are, the better golfer you will be. And once I can convince a client that achieving these things often doesn't involve a swinging motion but actually requires moving some weight, then we can start to make some real progress.

Nearly every golfer who goes to a gym or works out in any capacity now tries to find "golf-fitness" exercises to incorporate into his routine. In most cases, he swings a dumbbell like a golf club, does some sort of rotation with the pulleys, or uses a medicine ball to mimic his swing. He also tends to do a lot of stretching, foam rolling, and resistance-band work, again, focusing on rotation.

While some of these can play out as very effective when done right and in conjunction with other exercises, a big concern of mine comes when very little true **strength**-work gets incorporated into the typical golfer's routine.

I don't know why, but many of the golfers whom I meet seem afraid to actually put some weight in their hands or on a bar and do some real work when it comes to lifting.

While there is a definite need to incorporate rotational and "triplanar" (exercises in all 3 planes of motion) exercises in your programs, there are also many other components that should be included in a solid program. If you want to perform at your best, you need to get as strong, lean (okay, this may be debateable), fast, and powerful as possible. This means over-all, not just in regards to rotation.

Do you think a guy training for the Olympic hammer throw does rotation exercises all day? Absolutely not. He uses squatting, deadlifting, and other compound exercises to gain as much brute strength as possible. Why? Because every ounce of that strength helps to generate the rotational force that lets him hurl that hammer through the air.

The same mentality can benefit the development of your golf power. While you don't need to run out to sign up for the nearest strong man competition, I encourage you to start looking at your fitness program as other athletes do.

Hockey players don't just work on the slap shot motion (in fact, I have never seen an NHL player work on that in the gym); quarterbacks don't just practice throwing, and baseball players don't just work on hitting mechanics. So why does a golfer think everything he does should look like a swing? The athletes in other sports realize that they need to make a place for strength/conditioning and a place for the technical work.

STRENGTH x SPEED = POWER

While golf is a game of finesse and touch, it is also very much becoming a game of **power** more than ever before. And by definition (actually the true definition is **Power = Work/Time** but it's often stated "**Strength x Speed = Power**"), the only success in increasing your power comes when you increase speed (**time**) and/or increase strength (**work**-which basically means the amount of weight moved)—both of which can occur in the gym very easily with the right combination of exercises.

Let's take for granted that we understand how much of a factor the mental game and the skill/short game have on a player's success and let's just focus on the explosive component instead. From a fitness perspective, we obviously can have the most impact on this. Yes, a workout program can also have components to help the mental and skill side, but strength, speed, and power are our "bread and butter."

Usually, about this time some intimidation sets in, but don't worry; you don't have to fear adding some weight to your exercises. I'm not talking about walking into the gym tomorrow, loading up the bar with 225-lbs. and ripping out five sets of clean and jerks.

As with anything, you have to approach this in a realistic and intelligent manner. If you've never really lifted weights, obviously you should have some guidance. Find someone who can show you the right way to do some of the more important lifts like squats and deadlifts. If you do have some experience, but haven't done it in a while, start slowly and progress appropriately.

It's more about progressing with the weight so you can increase your muscles' ability to handle and create tension. As your muscles get stronger, they can create more force. More force leads to more speed and power.

By doing more demanding exercises, you teach your body to move and react more efficiently. This efficiency leads to better body-awareness, faster swing-speeds, and more consistent swings. All good things, right?

And even better news, as your body gets used to handling a little weight and can perform many different exercises through the proper range of motion and with resistance, you will also notice your flexibility increase.

Again, I emphasize that the exercises have to be performed properly, stressing full range-of-motion and emphasis on quality of tempo and posture. When performed with these points in mind, the extra weight will actually help improve the motion, rather than cause you to become less flexible as the myths would have us believe.

WHAT EXERCISES SHOULD I BE DOING?

The idea of adding weight doesn't have to sound scary. And it definitely shouldn't be limited to a population of "young people." Unfortunately, that is what most of my older clients proclaim the first time I show them some of the exercises that I have prescribed. (The truth of the matter is that the older population may need the weight training more than the youth simply for long-term health and balance benefits).

Many people don't realize that they can handle added resistance simply because they haven't tried in the past. Once you realize that it's okay to grab the 20-lb. weight instead of the pink 3-lb. one without hurting yourself, you become mentally ready to make progress in your training program. Our bodies are amazing and are much more resilient that we give them credit for at times. But without challenging them, they are not encouraged to adapt. Simply testing the limits from time to time can create tremendous results.

Now it's time to find some exercises that give you a little more return on your investment. Some examples of these include squats, overhead squats, deadlifts, pull ups, split squats, back extensions, hamstring curls, and many more. The key is to constantly ask yourself,

"What do I want to achieve with this program?"

"What exercises can I use to achieve this goal?"

"Which ones will give me the most efficient workout?"

Every exercise must have a purpose. If you put it into your program just to fill a space rather than for a specific purpose, rethink it and change it if necessary.

And, of course, if you see this as new territory for you and you feel a little intimidated, that's cool. In fact, that's normal. In this case, I encourage you to take the time and make the effort to find someone who can show you how and what to do to get on the right track.

If you don't know where to start, contact me at **18STRONG.com**, and let me know that you read the book and you need a little guidance. If I have a resource in your area, we'll get you connected.

BOGEY-PROOF ACTION TIPS FOR CHALLENGING YOURSELF

- Commit to pushing yourself and trust in the fact that you generally can do much more than you think possible in just about every aspect of life, including in your workouts.

- Write down every exercise and weight that you perform in your workouts. Then try to get a little stronger each week.

- Be sure you are including "bigger" exercises in your routine, such as squats, deadlifts, pull ups, lunges, etc., and try adding some real weight to them. You'll be surprised at what you can actually do.

- If you can't get comfortable doing this or starting down this path on your own, find a well respected coach who can assess you and guide you in the right direction.

Find these tips and more at BogeyProofWorkout.com/resources.

SMARTER CARDIO

This section of the book may turn out as the one where you actually like what I have to say.

Why?

Because I am going to tell you to

"Get Off the Elliptical Machine!"

That's right. Probably not what you expected. Or, maybe, if you've read or heard any of my advice in the past, you might already know that I'm not a big fan of cardio for the golfer. Or let me qualify that, traditional cardio as most of us know it.

Do you find that surprising, coming from a fitness professional?

For some reason, especially here in the United States, a very large population has literally become "**addicted to cardio.**"

When someone says he needs to lose weight (and by that, he really means he needs to lose **FAT**), what usually comes out of his mouth?

"I really should do more cardio."

Let's clarify. By "cardio," what this individual implies is the act of getting on the treadmill or elliptical for 30-45 minutes to burn some calories in an effort to counteract the crappy food he's eating.

Despite what you've previously heard or read, this type of cardio has to rank as one of the least effective ways of losing weight, getting leaner, and improving your golf game. Let me ask you a couple of questions here to illustrate my point.

1. When was the last time you had to jog for 30 minutes on the golf course?

2. How many people do you know who have done the treadmill (or elliptical) for years and still haven't lost the weight or made any significant change to the way their bodies look?

3. Do you think in any way that jogging at a slow to medium pace can make your swing faster and more explosive?

4. Did you know several ways exist to make your body more efficient at burning calories (and fat) that take only a fraction of the time that one of these traditional "cardio" sessions takes?

Hopefully, these questions have you intrigued, and you want to hear of a better, faster, and more efficient way to achieve your fitness performance and physique goals.

Let's get started by talking about what you currently do.

CARDIO AS YOU KNOW IT

I'm not sure whose idea it was to start jogging long distances for fun, but he or she is a sick individual.

Of course, I say that in jest as I have several friends and family members who are runners and they simply love doing their half and full marathons—which I think is awesome. Anytime someone decides to push and challenge him/herself to achieve a physical goal, I'm all for it.

But somewhere along the line, people got the idea that running was the only real way you could get lean and burn calories. This then led to the creation of the treadmill which allowed you to get the same "benefits" from conveniently running in your home, the gym, hotel, etc. A good idea, I admit. But I think we've taken it too far.

The popularity of the treadmill led to an increase in all "cardio" pieces such as more sophisticated stationary bikes, ellipticals, arc trainers, and even Tony Little's **Gazelle®.** (You remember that guy, right? He made mega-millions on those silly things!)

Now you can't go to a gym without walking into a sea of "cardio" equipment with flat screen TVs mounted on them (the TVs alone should tell you there is something wrong with this situation).

This idea of "cardio" has now devolved, and we've gone from running races and pushing the body to the limit to walking at a slow pace on a treadmill and reading magazines while riding the stationary bike.

That is not my idea of a "fat-burning machine."

In fact, it might be just the opposite. This kind of exercise could actually KEEP the fat on you.

YOUR CARDIO IS MAKING YOU FAT

At our most primitive level, we have our greatest instinct: to survive. From the days of the caveman to now, to protect itself from harm remains the number one thing our body is designed to do.

In order for this to happen, our bodies have amazingly adapted and become more efficient, especially when it comes to exercise and fat loss.

The body's job is to utilize the least amount of effort when faced with a challenge. When the body gets exposed to repetitive, long-duration exercise—i.e., cardio—the body rapidly adapts to the stresses in order to expend as little energy as possible.

In most cases you would find this good, but when you try to lose weight, you want to expend as much energy (i.e., fat) as you can.

So after you do the same cardio routine for a short period of time, your body figures out what is expected of it and readily adapts to reduce the stress, to expend less energy, and, thus, lessens the burning of fat.

So at first you might notice some good changes in your body composition and weight when introducing a new treadmill routine, but, soon enough, you hit a plateau, and the progress halts. This also rings true for doing the same weights-routine for years on end.

The next time you step into the gym, look around at the people in there. Most of them are doing the same routine that they have done for years. And, as a result, most of them look pretty much the same as they have since they started their routines a long, long time ago.

As another great example of the inefficiency of long-duration cardio, look at the different body types of individuals who run marathons. You'll find a wide array of sizes and shapes. This is great because it means that people of all backgrounds and skill levels can achieve the goal of running a marathon, but that doesn't mean that they get the most optimal fat-burning cardio from their training (which of course, may or may not be their ultimate goal).

Obviously, these people all put in some major hours on the road or treadmill. But has all that cardio done much in regards to burning fat and losing weight? If that was the original intention, then I think they've missed the mark.

And in a sport like golf, where there is not much stress placed on the cardiopulmonary system (your heart and lungs), but there is a lot of need for explosive power, I would argue that traditional cardio is not very targeted toward the needs of your game.

YOU CALL THAT A SPRINT?

Now that you have a slight understanding that long-duration cardio at a low to moderate effort level is NOT the most efficient way to burn fat, let's look at one method that has been proven to be EXTREMELY effective: SPRINTS.

When I say "sprints," what's the first thing that comes to mind? Running on a track? Probably. But that's not exactly what I'm talking about. Well, it is, and it isn't.

When I say "sprints," I am talking about some form of exercise where you exert a maximum amount of effort for a short period of time. It doesn't necessarily have to include running. While running sprints on a track may stand as one of the BEST ways of doing this, you have endless options. I'll list a few examples:

- bike sprints

- shuttle runs

- running steps

- running on the treadmill

- jumping rope

- battle ropes

- mountain climbers

- swimming

- golf swings . . .

And this is just a short list. Bottom line, it has to be something that you can do SAFELY, with good form, but at **MAXIMUM** effort.

Since we mentioned it above, let's take running sprints on the track as an example. First, to give you a visual, I want you to envision a sprinter and then envision a typical marathon runner.

If you need help visualizing, simply google "sprinter vs. marathoner" in Google images and look at the side-by-side comparisons.

Which one of these looks more efficient in burning body-fat? Which one looks like he or she would be more powerful and explosive? Without question, it is the sprinter.

I know what you might think: I am a golfer. I have no reason to "sprint" on the golf course. How on earth could that help me?

You have a valid question.

Simply put, there are clear cut benefits from sprints, including:

- burning fat

- improving testosterone-levels

- improving insulin-sensitivity
- developing cardiovascular endurance
- creating more speed
- creating more power.

As you can tell, all of these are not golf-related, but they are all "life"-related. By including these in your weekly routine, you will be doing yourself a big favor, not only for power in your swing, but also in living a healthier life.

For more information on the benefits of sprint-intervals, I encourage you to listen to the interview I did with Dr. Mark Smith on the **18STRONG Podcast** (http://18STRONG.com/mark-smith/).

You can also find Dr. Smith's research paper on "Super High Intensity Intervals" in your free resources at www.BogeyProofWorkout.com/resources.

Now that you understand the benefits of these sprints, I'm sure you want to know the best way to incorporate them into your workout.

My first suggestion: don't overcomplicate it.

You simply want two ingredients when sprinting . . .

MAXIMAL EFFORT and **REST.**

By "maximal effort" I mean all out, 100% effort, and by "rest" I mean completely chilling out, doing nothing, or next to nothing.

A big mistake made when trying to achieve a high intensity sprint-interval workout occurs when an individual tries to go too hard for too long without enough rest in between sets.

The sprinting should last no more than 60 seconds; otherwise, the body can no longer maintain maximum output and will start to break down in form.

Per Dr. Smith's protocol in his paper, I often use a one-minute sprint to a 3-4-minute rest break ratio when doing a pure sprint-training workout.

If you find yourself short on time and can't get a devoted sprint-day, I would recommend mixing them into your strength-training workouts. A word of caution here, though: if you do any "primary lifts" (the big heavy lifts) like those we discussed earlier, I would insert the sprints after those lifts or at the end of your workout.

You don't want to rob your nervous system and muscles of energy before doing a complex lift because that could cause you to sacrifice your form and contribute to an injury.

In many situations, I will add in sprint intervals at the end of a client's workout, or I will add them in on a circuit-day when we do more of a high-rep/low-weight workout, not on a heavy-lifting day unless we do them at the very end.

You can also play around with the times a bit. For example, you could do sprints on the treadmill at a slight incline and challenging speed for 20 seconds, rest for 10 seconds, and do that up to three times. Then take a longer rest break before doing that again or going to a different exercise.

To help you sort some of this out, I've created a few sprint templates for you to try. Again, just go to your free downloadable resources at www. BogeyProofWorkout.com/resources to get access.

Now, I know sprints are never the most appealing component to add to your repertoire so I've got another suggestion that might appeal more to those who enjoy hitting the weights more than the track.

THE BARBELL VS. THE TREADMILL

If you needed to lose some fat, increase your strength/power and had to choose between access to a treadmill or a set of weights, which would you pick?

I would pick the weights, 100 times out of 100.

"Why," you ask?

Because I know for a fact that I can get more "work" done in a much shorter time and more efficiently by using weights properly than I can on a treadmill.

I know, I just told you how beneficial sprints are for burning fat and gaining power, and that is 100% true. But I use that as a secondary tool when it comes to designing a program for someone who wants be as lean, fast and powerful as they can be.

Several reasons for this include:

1. Lifting weights (especially heavy weights) creates more stress on the body than endurance exercise.

2. Weight-training with sufficient loads impacts the body's muscle fibers, both Type I (slow twitch) and Type II (fast twitch), which promotes the building of lean muscle mass. Lean muscle leads to more efficient energy-burning (i.e., fat-burning).

3. "Steady State Cardio" (endurance-style cardio) inhibits the body's ability to build muscle, thus lessening its ability to burn fat and get stronger.

4. The effects of weight-training continue after the workout to burn calories, whereas steady state cardio does not have nearly as long of a "post-workout effect."

5. A greater hormonal response comes from weight-training. In particular, testosterone, growth hormone, and cortisol levels can be dramatically increased as a result of weight-training, more so than with steady state cardio. All three of these benefit you in increasing lean muscle mass and improving body-composition and power-output.

As you can see, many reasons exist to choose weight over cardio, no matter what you have as your goals.

If you want to try for more power, more speed, to burn fat, to gain lung capacity, etc., all of these get impacted significantly with the proper use of a weight-training routine.

So, when I build a program for a client, I look at his training level, his capacity for movement, previous injuries, and ability to move functionally. Then, based on my findings, I will create a weights-based program FIRST, accompanied by some corrective exercises.

If he is a very dedicated individual with enough time on his hands, I will then include some sort of sprints into the program as needed. But as my first objective, I want to get him moving better and start building some functional strength.

Once he starts to show improvements in that, I will add weight, as tolerated, to begin working on specific goals.

If the individual already has some experience in the gym, this process can move much faster, and we will start taxing his system with SAFE but challenging weights in order to achieve his goals.

Speaking of goals, I think you need to move on to the most important concept in this book. If you've hung in here this long, I know you have a commitment to not only improving your golf game, but also to learning how to make your body a more efficient machine. This will not only benefit you on the course, but also in every facet of your life.

This next chapter reveals the fastest way I have found to achieve any goal in life, fitness-related or not.

BOGEY-PROOF ACTION TIPS FOR BETTER CARDIO

- Stop doing "steady-state," long-duration cardio sessions.
- Incorporate sprints-intervals into your program to increase your metabolic rate without hindering your ability to gain lean muscle.
- Opt for the weights vs. the treadmill when looking for a more effective and efficient way to lose fat.

Find these tips and more at BogeyProofWorkout.com/resources.

THE ULTIMATE GAME CHANGER #7

really believe that this ranks as one of the most effective and time tested strategies one can employ to achieve a goal in the least amount of time.

And that strategy is:

Find someone to help guide you through this journey.

No matter who you are, what you do, and how good you think you are at something, everyone can use a mentor or coach. Someone needs to guide you on your journey to greatness, challenge you to do things you think you can't, and prevent you from doing things you shouldn't.

Intellectually, we all know this, and, in some areas of your life, you already do this: you probably have a financial planner, an accountant, etc. Why? To help you, to guide you, to make sure you don't do something stupid or get off track, right?

Well, I've seen lots of people get off track or follow less than great information when it comes to fitness. Between fad-diets, insane cardio powerlifting bootcamps, incorrect form and misunderstanding of exercises, lots of people put themselves at risk in the gym.

And as mentioned earlier, the fact that simply having someone watching over you and holding you accountable will get you off your butt and in the gym more than any other incentive I've seen.

INFORMATION OVERLOAD

We have access to as much information as we would ever need right at the tips of our fingers. You can find any exercise, diet plan, workout, or golf tip with a few strokes of the keys on your laptop. So why would anyone need a mentor?

It is precisely that infinite amount of accessibility that makes it more important than ever to find someone whom you can trust. So much information floats around out there that it's often impossible to distinguish the BS from good stuff.

For that reason, you should invest in a trusted advisor; someone who can sift through all of the misinformation and shortcut your learning process. I assume that you want nothing but the best and most effective plan to achieve your goals as soon as possible.

The most effective way to do that is to let someone show you how to do it. You want someone who has walked that walk or, even better, has shown countless other people to do what you look to do for yourself.

We do exactly that at **18STRONG.com** and with our athletes at our training facility. We realize so much bogus information churns around out there that we feel our job includes sifting through the garbage and delivering the most pertinent and effective techniques/lessons for you to implement into your program.

FIND A MENTOR NOT JUST A TRAINER

Take note that I said to find a "mentor" or "coach," and not necessarily a "trainer." There is a big difference. Not all trainers are meant to be (or fit to be) coaches/mentors. By my definition, a trainer typically **helps people exercise**. He/she tells you what exercises to do, counts your reps, and might even correct your form on occasion.

A coach/mentor **teaches you HOW** to exercise and train properly. He/she gives you guidance on the things you need to do to make it to the next level. His concern lies more with the plan and progress of your program than whether you got in a "good sweat today."

A mentor has an end goal in mind—**YOUR end goal**. And he wants to empower you to get there, whether it's in the gym together or on your own. A trainer also has your best interests at heart (hopefully), but the plan relies on his walking you from exercise to exercise, counting your reps for you, and telling you when to come back next week.

Let me give you an example. In our facility, we have lots of young athletes coming through the door. If we used the "trainer mentality," would the kids get better while training with us? (Yes, of course: we are really good☺!)

But let me ask you this. If we did not teach them HOW to properly lift, perform their corrective exercises, and condition themselves while they work out ON THEIR OWN, would they get any better when they leave for college and have to go to the gym on their own? Some will; but many won't.

A mentor and coach teaches the individual "to fish" as the old parable goes. You need to have the ability to exercise ON YOUR OWN, design your own programs, work on your flexibility, and SELF-CORRECT your swing. Your trainer can't hold your hand when you work out at home or while traveling.

The same goes for your swing-coach/golf game—not to mention that, unless you have unlimited funds and all the time in the world to spend at the gym, it takes more than just your three sessions a week to really get in shape and improve your game.

So I offer my suggestion. Go to **18STRONG.com** and sign up to get our emails so we can help you along your journey. This will take care of the next step in getting your program off to a good start. With access to the greatest coaches in the world and the stories from players who have reached the highest level, you will not only get top class INFORMATION, but hopefully INSPIRATION as well.

Second, I would highly recommend finding a QUALIFIED professional who can assess your personal needs and get you on the right track. If you don't know where to find one, contact me, and I will see if I know any-one in your area. By the time you read this, we may even have an online coaching program set up over at **18STRONG.com**.

Also, the Titleist Performance Institute website (MyTPI.com) is a good place to start as they have a database of certified instructors across the nation, and are the leaders in producing quality information on golf per-formance for coaches all over the world.

BOGEY-PROOF ACTION TIPS FOR FINDING A MENTOR

- Go to **18STRONG.com** and sign up for our emails and start learning.

- If you haven't already, download all of your free resources from the book and start with your training program: www.BogeyProofWorkout.com/resources.

- DO NOT read everything you can find on the internet and take it as reputable information.

- Find information only from sources you trust and stick with them. Following a consistent philosophy is key to producing results over time your training.

- If you feel more comfortable working directly with someone, find a coach who has worked with and had success with many others before you.

Find these tips and more at BogeyProofWorkout.com/resources.

MY TWO CENTS . . .

Y ou probably wouldn't guess it just by looking at guys like Phil Mickelson, Rickie Fowler, or Bubba Watson, but when you watch them swing, you realize how much power they can harness in their golf swing. In my opinion, we have begun seeing just the beginning of a new era of ridiculous power. If I had to put money on it, I would venture to bet that over the next ten years, we will start seeing even more of a shift in the fitness level, size, strength, and speed of the golfers on tour.

The trend in any sport that starts to introduce fitness and sports-performance leads toward bigger, stronger athletes. Look at basketball and baseball over the past 20 years. The shift in golf has begun. We already see it with guys like Tiger Woods, Rory McIlroy, Jason Day, Jordan Spieth, etc.

While golf will never require the same level of strength and size as a sport like football or hockey, I believe we already can see quite a few advantages in the game for the guys that have more power off the tee. Not to mention that the guys with a higher fitness level are less likely to break down physically in the later rounds and over the course of the season, which definitely impacts ball-striking abilities.

For those who say, "Fitness isn't important in golf," because guys like John Daly, Kevin Stadler, and other portly fellows have won on tour, I give you my philosophy and argument: What if those guys were in awesome shape? How much better would they golf and how much more longevity would they have in the game? (Here is where I throw John Daly back at them!) I venture to say that they would play quite a bit better and, at least, would stay in contention more often because their bodies would not tend to break down.

Another way to think about it is this: Who do you think would win more often in a match between a **fat and out-of-shape** Jordan Spieth versus a **fit-and-trim** Jordan Spieth? The fit Jordan would, of course—maybe not every time, but I would bet more times than not.

I do not say that getting in great shape will make YOU or anyone else a great golfer. I DO believe that it can make you a BETTER golfer. And I will definitely say that taking a great golfer and getting him/her in better shape for his/her golf game will make him/her an even greater golfer.

Golf has the reputation of a game of mental strength, finesse, and explosive power, all wrapped up in one. And it takes all three to stay great at this game. Getting really strong in one or two of these areas can make you a very good golfer, but the guys who succeed the most have all three.

In my opinion, we must realize the extreme importance of taking advantage of the tangible things over which we have control. In many respects, our fitness has to rank as one of those things. By simply assessing what you need to improve and knowing what strengths you have, you can take that information and make significant changes and improvements to your game relatively quickly.

CONCLUSION
WHAT TO DO NEXT . . .

Congratulations on being in a very small minority of people who know what you now know! If you actually have read all the way to this point and didn't just skip ahead to get the "cliff notes" version, you now know more about a well constructed golf-fitness program than many of the personal trainers and golf pros I have met over the years.

And you definitely know more than I did when I started working with golfers several years ago!

But we have a problem. Now that you have this information, you can never go back. You know too much to have a mediocre program anymore.

You now have a duty to implement these principles immediately and create a GREAT Golf Fitness program.

In order to make this as easy as possible, I again want to provide you with a clear-cut action plan to get going on this TODAY! So I'll give you an even easier and more concise action plan for you to get moving on.

1. **Plan It Out**
   - Create a workout program (or find one) to follow for the next four to six weeks. (You'll find one in your resources at www.BogeyProofWorkout.com/resources.)
   - Track your progress.
   - Find a partner if you want to make it more entertaining and really create some accountability.

2. **Emphasize Balance**
   - Remember to make sure you work balance into your program whether you do so in every workout or, at the least, in your schedule for the week. (If you use the workout we've put together, we've got you covered.)
   - Train yourself like an athlete, not just a guy that swings a club.

3. **Eat Better**
   - Create an eating lifestyle, not a diet.
   - Eat more protein, eat more veggies, and EARN your carbs.
   - Start using a post-workout shake (with or without carbs, depending on your goals).
   - Determine whether taking a multivitamin and fish oil is right for you.

4. **Work Out Better**
   - Do every exercise with perfect posture.
   - Determine the goal of each exercise or workout (i.e., strength, speed, energy burn, etc.).
   - Give each exercise a tempo that you HAVE to follow.

5. **Use Heavier Weights**
   - Use bigger, compound-exercises to maximize your time in the gym (squats, deadlifts, presses, lunges, pull ups, etc.).
   - Challenge yourself.

6. **Use Your Cardio Wisely**
   - Use weights to increase your ability to burn fat and get leaner and more powerful.
   - Include sprints instead of long duration "old-school" cardio.

7. **Find a Mentor**
   - You can choose a coach whom you physically see in person or a resource, like myself and **18STRONG.com**, where you know you can go to get answers.
   - Use the mentor to create a plan that is right for you.
   - Enjoy the Journey.

THANK YOU

F irst and foremost, I want to thank YOU for taking the time to read this book. It took quite a while to get all of these thoughts on paper, and I'm very gratified to know that someone made it to the end, hopefully with a stronger knowledge-base than when you started.

While this book contains a lot of information, just remember that you now have a better understanding of creating and/or following a fitness/strength-training program than the majority of the population does. Don't try to overcomplicate it. The only mistake you can make lies in not acting on what you've learned.

I would also like to take this opportunity to thank several people in my life who have contributed in one way or another to this book becoming a reality. First and foremost, my wife Susan and my kids, Sam, Riese, and Grant. I know I spent hours and hours in front of the computer while complete chaos went on around me. Thank you for holding down the fort. I love you all.

I also have quite a few friends and colleagues who made this possible in one way or another. I intend to thank you all personally so I won't go into details here, but I did want to list some names to publicly recognize how much I appreciate you. In no particular order, these are the people whom I can't thank enough for their support of me and **18STRONG**: Tony Soaib, Jon Benne, Ryan McMullen, Nick Mueller, Justin Tupper, T.E. Frances, Adam Stevenson, Mitch Sadowsky, Jason Glass, Lance Gill, Dr. Bhrett McCabe, Dr. Austin Panter, Clint Howard, Ali Gilbert, Michael Manavian, Nick Chertock, Chris Lutes, Lindsay Manion, TJ Preuss, Tim Besmer, Dr. Mark Smith, Matt Kopsky, Shawn and Anne Stevenson, every single guest on the **18STRONG Podcast**, and, of course, my Mom and Dad.

A MASSIVE THANK YOU, to the small group of people that were kind enough to read the raw draft early on and give me some very valuable, REAL, and constructive feedback, I want to acknowledge all of you. This project came together thanks to you:

David Keusenkothen, Tony Soaib, TJ Preuss, Wes Altice, Elizabeth Sander, Juan Gutierrez, Andrew Lietzow, Greg Barker, Adrian Sesto, Jadel Menard, Brian Fitzpatrick, Rene Cammarata, Wayne "Gooch" Yamaguchi and my lovely wife Susan Pelizzaro. Your feedback definitely made a huge impact on the final version of this book!

ABOUT
THE AUTHOR

'm Jeff Pelizzaro. I am a physical therapist and golf fitness professional in St. Louis, Missouri. I didn't grow up playing golf; in fact, I didn't really play golf much until I started working with golfers on a regular basis in 2008.

I grew up playing pretty much all sports, but my passion was soccer, which I played into college.

When I realized I wasn't going to be the next David Beckham, I decided I should probably start focusing on my studies, which led me to get my Masters of Physical Therapy from Rockhurst University in Kansas City.

I've traveled a long journey from my first position as a clinical therapist at a hospital in St. Louis to now, but after working with thousands of patients and clients on every level (spinal cord injuries, amputations, sports injuries, professional athletes, etc.), I've come to realize that the body is an amazing piece of equipment.

I don't have all of the answers, but I've figured a few things out over the years. What I've put in this book summarizes the fundamentals of what I have found to work extremely well for nearly every individual with whom I've worked, interviewed or connected in some way over the years.

I seriously encourage you to implement these strategies. I personally guarantee that the changes you seek will come. You just have to trust the process!

All the best.

Jeff

Train Hard. Practice Smart. Play Better Golf.

Made in the USA
San Bernardino, CA
15 December 2016